JESUS SAYS TO YOU

Books by Daniel A. Poling

Mothers of Men 1914

Huts in Hell 1918

Report on Steel Strike of 1919: Inter-Church World Movement
(two volumes, arranged and edited with Robert Bruère) 1920

Learn to Live 1923

What Men Need Most 1923

An Adventure in Evangelism 1925

The Furance (novel) 1925

John of Oregon (novel) 1926

Radio Talks to Young People 1926

Dr. Poling's Radio Talks 1927

The Heretic (novel) 1928

Youth and Life 1929

Between Two Worlds (novel) 1930
(reissued as The Romance of Jesus)

John Barleycorn: His Life and Letters (novel) 1933

Youth Marches 1937

Fifty-two Story Sermons for Children 1940

Opportunity Is Yours 1940

A Treasury of Best Loved Hymns 1942

A Preacher Looks at War 1943

Your Daddy Did Not Die 1944

A Treasury of Great Sermons 1944

Faith Is Power for You 1950

Prayers for the Armed Forces 1950

The Glory and Wonder of the Bible (with Dr. Henry Thomas) 1954

Your Questions Answered with Comforting Counsel 1956

Mine Eyes Have Seen 1959

Jesus Says to You 1961

JESUS
SAYS TO YOU

His Eternal Wisdom and Its Meaning Today

DANIEL A. POLING

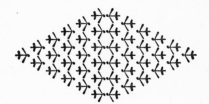

McGRAW-HILL BOOK COMPANY, INC.

New York   Toronto   London

JESUS SAYS TO YOU

Library of Congress Catalog Card Number: 60-53354

50379

CONTENTS

INTRODUCTION

The Christian Church is the Resurrection Church, the Christian faith is a Resurrection faith and experience, and these forty chapters are Resurrection messages for you and for me. Jesus said and says, "I am the Resurrection and the Life," and He gave and gives as the reason for His coming that "They"—even the humblest of those about Him—"might have life and have it more abundantly."

The biography of Jesus may be comprehended in five words: "He went about doing good." In seven words the Apostle Paul gave us the most concise and at the same time most comprehensive appraisal of His ministry: "The same yesterday, and today, and forever." My comments in this book will not surpass these statements for brevity, but they will be found to deal with the same essential matter as I have experienced it personally in the course of a lifetime: the infinite good that Jesus set in motion by thought, word, and action, and the timeless authority of His message and His methods.

DANIEL A. POLING

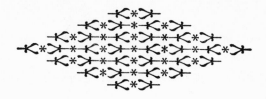

1. THE GREAT "I MUST"

J ESUS SAYS: *How is it that ye sought me? Wist ye not that I must be about my Father's business?*

LUKE 2:49

These are the words of a twelve-year-old boy, the lad Jesus, spoken in the Temple at Jerusalem when Mary and Joseph, His parents, after an anxious search, found Him talking, "sitting in the midst of the doctors, both hearing them, and asking them questions." With Jesus it was the great compulsion, the inevitable "I must." Twenty years, the "hidden years," would elapse before He would begin His brief but epochal public ministry of three years, but already He knew what He *must do*. Already His was a committed life. He would grow in "stature and in favour with God and man." He would mature, but at twelve the drive of His destiny had possessed Him, and "I must be about my Father's business" was the only answer that He gave His parents when, with so great and natural a concern, they found Him when He had become separated from

I

them on the return trip to Nazareth after the annual Passover feast.

Perhaps no person ever really lives, enjoys life to the full, who has not known in some measure at least the great "I must." I know a man who, as a young collegian, was ambitious to be an athlete, a middle-distance runner. Beyond ambition he had little to commend him to the coach and trainer, but he persisted. He spent long hours on the track alone. He followed instructions to the letter. He absorbed information and learned by watching others. Again and again he said, as he rubbed another man down after a meet, "I am going to do it. I've got to do it." And he did. He became consistently the fastest man on his college team and a breaker of records. And this great "I must" followed him, commanded him as an engineer. He became a builder and a leader in his profession, first in the Southwest and then in the far North.

During one of my city pastorates, a high school graduate came to the university with which I was closely associated. It was necessary for him to work his way through. Becoming restless while he waited for the institution to give him a contact for a possible job, he started out on his own. The city was strange, but within four hours he had turned up three student jobs. With one for himself, he returned to the registrar's office with two for others. During his four college years he was active in the YMCA and his own church. He drove ahead both purposefully and expectantly. He did not graduate at the head or even near the head of his class, but he finished creditably. Today he is one of the younger presidents of a successful life-insurance company. Always the philosophy of this boy and man has been "I must." Not for himself alone and his family but for others and to make his life count for the most.

During a college summer vacation, I worked in The Dalles, Oregon, where my uncle was minister of the historic First Congregational Church. With him as my guide, I visited a recluse from the East, an aged man who had built for himself high above the town and the Columbia River a cabin that overlooked the world. He had carried the boards up a trail he had made and enlarged a natural cave that was the first unit of his rude but comfortable dwelling. Once, when my uncle sought to bring him down into the town where he could receive care and hospitalization, the old man shook his head and said, "No, I have everything here. Everything I now love and care for. I have the sunrise and the sunset, the river and the broad lands beyond, the city below and the high sky. I have the world and the universe—all mine. No, my good friend, I have everything and I *must* stay."

And so it was from his cave and cabin that they carried the old man down to bury him. From the high command of the great "I must" of Jesus to the aged recluse on the mountain who was at the end of his journey, it is the same compulsion— life's great "I must."

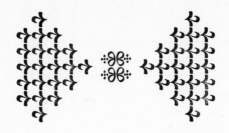

2. THE CALL

JESUS SAYS: *Follow me....*
MATTHEW 4:19

When Jesus came down to Lake Galilee and called two young fishermen who were brothers, Andrew and Simon Peter, He was already in full stride toward His fated destiny—the Roman Cross of torture and shame, but a triumph that would "turn the world upside down."

"Follow me," He said. And Andrew and Simon left their nets and followed Him. Behind Jesus on that day were soul-shaking experiences. He had been baptized in the Jordan by His cousin John, and for forty days He had fasted and prayed in the wilderness. And it is written that in the wilderness He was "tempted of the devil."

The baptismal scene is associated with the miraculous event in which the heavens opened and the Voice cried "This is my beloved Son, in whom I am well pleased: hear ye him." From that announcement Jesus went forth in the brave beginnings of

4

His ministry, and it was almost immediately thereafter that He experienced the ordeal of His Satanic temptation. "Follow me," He said to Andrew and Simon, "and I will make you fishers of men." But the heart of that challenging call is "Follow me, and I will make you...." The unique promise of Jesus, unique in time and space, and—finally—unique in its impact upon eternity: "I will make you...."

Jesus took raw human material (and very raw it was), remade it, and with it remade the lives of men and women. Then, with remade men and women ("new creatures," the Scriptures call them) He remade life itself. How revolutionary this process was is demonstrated in the life of Simon Peter, Andrew's brother. Uncouth, unlettered, quarrelsome, and headstrong, this Galilean fisherman who first denied and then repented, finally followed Jesus to a triumphant death. He became the human head of a Christian Church that has enfolded in its spiritual embrace countless millions of all races, tongues, and colors. He is today the trumpeter who sounds over the ages to all Christians of every creed and clime: "Thou art the Christ, the Son of the Living God."

"Follow me," Jesus said to the brothers by Galilee, and in speaking to them He spoke beyond them to all others who will give ear to His words. For He speaks as never man spoke. The Apostle Paul, in his letter to the Hebrews, declares: "Jesus Christ the same yesterday, and today, and forever."

My young friend Dr. Tom Dooley, a medical missionary of the Roman Catholic Church in the jungles of Viet Nam, hard against Red China, two years ago came home from his hospital to be operated on for a malignancy. Scarcely were the incisions closed than this young man was off again to his frontier rendezvous to reassure and comfort his tragic patients by revealing to them in his own person the sustaining grace of the Great Physician. "Come with me and I will make you...," Jesus said to Tom Dooley.

In the swamps and along the sullen rivers of Ecuador, the Aucas—perhaps the most primitive of all South American jungle tribes—five years ago murdered five young American missionaries who came to them with love and only love. The Americans died as died their nameless and unnumbered predecessors in this great work, the martyrs of the early Christian Church. But even as I write these lines, the Aucas have at last opened their villages and in a gesture of repentance and supplication have opened their hearts to the enduring message of these five young heroes who died together. Even though they have gone on, the missionaries continue to speak, and those whose ears are open hear the words spoken first beside Galilee: "Follow me, and I will make you...."

The promise Jesus made to Andrew and Simon Peter is timeless and universal. It is the same yesterday, today, and forever, and it was made to you and to me—to every man among us and to every woman. Jesus Christ has the answer to your every need and to mine. And He will remake us. Whatever our calling and our human relationships, He will remake us into the person we would become when we think and dream at our best.

3. THE METHOD OF
THE MASTER

Jesus SAYS: *Come and see.*

JOHN 1:39

Immediately after the baptism of Jesus by His cousin John in the Jordan River, as Jesus moved away from that profound occasion, two young men who had "seen and heard" followed Him. One of these was Andrew, Simon Peter's brother; the other was John, afterward known as "the beloved disciple." Turning on the two young men as they followed Him, Jesus asked, "What seek ye?" Perhaps to cover their confusion, they replied, "...where dwellest Thou?" And He answered—with a smile, I am sure—"Come and see."

It is written that they accepted the invitation and "abode with him that day." History completes the record. They never left Him! Throughout His brief life and after the Resurrection they remained by His side until they died their martyr deaths. They were His men. They could not escape Him.

Among the most dynamic words of Jesus were these three:

7

"Come and see." With His most characteristic invitation He bade those who followed Him with their questions to look into the matter for themselves. He never insulted the intelligence of His hearers or talked down to them. He respected their minds and their personalities, and ministered to their hungry and suffering bodies. Come and see for yourselves, He said. Watch Me at work. Study My methods; see what happens; know for yourselves—then decide for yourselves. He did not coerce men's minds; rather, on merit, He persuaded and won them. Then, of course, He commanded their allegiance; those who had "seen Him" followed Him through dangers, hardships, and human disasters to the death. But they knew what they were doing and, knowing, they would do no other. What held them was not mailed might but sacrificial love.

How timeless and enduring the invitation itself may be I have seen demonstrated repeatedly. On one occasion, following a citizenship address in a regular Sunday service, but to a special audience, I was tempted to pronounce the benediction without extending my customary invitation for a show of hands or a rising to feet if members of the congregation wished especially to be remembered in my closing prayer. Subconsciously, as I spoke—it *must* have been a subconscious thought —I prayed for guidance. I got the guidance; I extended the invitation and more than fifty men and women responded.

Among those whom I met at the close of that service was a young man who did not give me his name. He stated that he did not desire an interview; said he had been attending my services for three months; several times he had accepted my invitation and raised his hand; now he wished me to know that he felt the need of being remembered in a very special way. Two weeks later the young man came to me again and asked for a personal interview. We met the next afternoon. I told him, as is my custom, that he need give me no information concerning himself, that the interview was entirely in his hands, and I was at his command, but that, of course, my ability to help him would be largely determined by his willingness to trust me. Still he did not give me his name.

Two weeks later he came again and now he gave me his name, a proud name, and told me his story. He had been an Allied combat pilot in World War I under another flag than ours. He had been shot down and all but fatally wounded. Scars from burns still covered his body. As the result of both physical and nervous demoralization, the after-war period had been for him a time of torture. He had taken to drink and a dishonorable way of life, and he had shamed his people. A long story it was, but even now, after thirty-five years, I remember the details. Especially do I remember the happy ending that came as, through prayer, he found peace with power and went on to rehabilitate himself. I saw him often until he moved away, and one Christmas Sunday evening I found myself face to face with his joyful father and mother. Only those who have lived to experience such an hour of reconciliation can know the profoundly moving nature of that meeting.

For many years now this man has been successful in family life and in business, and the faith he found in a church on a New York avenue has kept him at the source of power. He found his faith because he was invited to find it, even as Jesus invited Andrew and John to come and see for themselves. That invitation of Jesus is still good for all the world. You have only to accept it.

4. WHY I BELIEVE IN ETERNAL LIFE

JESUS SAYS: ...*because I live, ye shall live also.*
JOHN 14:19

These words were spoken by Jesus to His disciples in the "upper room" after He and they had eaten the Last Supper together and just before He led them across the brook Kidron into the garden of Gethsemane where He was betrayed by Judas Iscariot. To me, these words are the sure promise of your life and my own beyond what for want of a better name we call "death."

And I believe in eternal life. My conviction that we live on became a vivid personal experience for me on a certain February morning in 1918. With an orderly I waited in the rain at the head of a communications trench north of Toul in France. A platoon from a United States machine-gun company was coming out. The lieutenant who brought up the rear stopped to inquire the way to the nearest canteen. He was sick and fever burned in his tired face. "Tonsilitis," he said as he leaned on his stick, "and trench foot." Then, pulling himself together, he stumbled on after his men. When he had gone a very short distance, a three-inch shell "let go" in the middle of his platoon. Hearing it coming, the orderly and I flung ourselves flat in the mud, and then at the screams of agony we hurried over to the wounded and dead. We looked after those who still needed the little we could do for them and we gathered up the fragments of the others.

There on that blood-soaked bit of French soil I experienced immortality. I knew that the lieutenant with the aching throat, the lad whose sick eyes had looked into mine as we talked a few moments before was not in what I had just picked up. I had not talked to *that*. But also I knew he was somewhere. I knew that there had been authority enough to begin his life, to carry it from his mother's womb to that awful end. Short of immortality I had the choice of just two conclusions: Either the creative authority had willed to leave that boy there in the blood and muck, willed to end him in such a sorry fashion, or the authority which could create was unable to continue, was helpless before the event.

Either conclusion was to me unacceptable and unreasonable. Both my heart and mind rejected them. I knew then, as I know now, that that young man did not stop where I picked up his battered body. He went on. It was not a debate then and is not now. It was an experience so real that it left me at the moment all but unconcerned about the pitifully broken body.

I had seen demonstrated the truth that Jesus told His disciples. Now I know that those whose forms I touch when only their forms remain, when to my touch there is no responsive pressure, have by the divine miracle survived. And I know where to find them! Also there is something more—that in you which is destined to live forever is alive now and will never die!

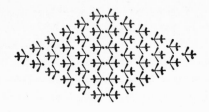

5. THE GREAT CONFESSION

Jesus says: ... *whom say ye that I am?*
MATTHEW 16:15

Jesus is forever answering questions. But now He asks a question. He had come with His disciples to the coast of Caesarea Philippi and with them, in a quiet place, He sat down to rest. It was then that He asked His searching question "Whom do men say that I the Son of man am?" They gave Him various replies. One said "John the Baptist," another said "Elias." Yet another said "Jeremias, or one of the prophets." But this composite answer did not satisfy the hungry heart of Jesus. He wished to know what these men who lived and worked with Him, who were His intimates, thought; and so He rephrased the question: "But whom say ye that I am?"

What an answer He got! It must have been to Jesus as the singing of many birds or as the sound of many waters, as up from the deep well of Peter's soul came the full words of a manly man: "Thou art the Christ, the Son of the living God."

After all it is not what the crowd thinks about a person, it is the judgment of one's intimates, it is the confession of one's closest friends that really counts. What does my daughter have to say? What does my son declare?

Peter's statement was his own confession of faith. It was more than a conclusion, and vastly more than a mere intellectual affirmation. It was the volcanic outburst of a progressive experience, an experience not yet complete, but an experience that was to shake the world as no earthquake or other physical upheaval ever has or ever will. Peter had actually experienced the fact to which he gave his testimony. He had come to know personally, to know in his innermost life, Jesus as the Son of the Living God.

Peter spoke the truth and lived it. History is his vindication, redeemed souls his confirmation. The richest experience in the life of any man or woman, the most profound and the holiest, is the experience of having the life and spirit of Jesus Christ possess the soul. And what is the experience in its outward manifestation? It is not a voice in the wilderness, but a life in the world. It is not an idea in the air, but feet on the ground going God's way in service to men and women and little children. It is not a fragile flower to be kept under glass, but a hardy plant to bear all manner of fruits in all manner of weather. Nothing we can say to God, no answer to His question "Whom say ye that I am?," no calling Him by great and dear names can ever take the place of the plain doing of His will. What is this experience? It is my life: Not what I believe but what I live; and that includes all that I believe.

Christianity needs today not truth-defenders but truth-demonstrators, and always the demonstration of truth is its best defense. Christianity needs now, as ever, men and women who reveal in little deeds of kindness done the life of Him whose briefest biography is "He went about doing good." Let me go further and say that Christianity needs you, who read these words, to answer, as Peter did with his life, Jesus' question.

David Metzger was a beloved professor and friend of my generation in a small Oregon college. He was a man of spiritual authority and spiritual achievement, yet chiefly he was a personality of vast human understanding. And as I now recall him, I know his source of power. He had an intimate friendship with Jesus Christ. He knew what Peter meant. That confession, "Thou art the Christ, the Son of the living God," was also the confession of David Metzger.

In time, he went to the Adirondacks to die. From his bed at Saranac Lake he wrote the letter that is still folded away between the covers of the Bible my mother gave me. This is one sentence from the letter:

"Brother Daniel, Jesus Christ is with me here and He is *everything*."

6. PRAY TO FORGIVE

JESUS SAYS: *And forgive us our debts, as we forgive our debtors.*
MATTHEW 6:12

These words are from the prayer Jesus taught His disciples in the days when He went about all Galilee, teaching and preaching the gospel of the Kingdom. The prayer has become the universal prayer of all Christians and, indeed, of many others who do not name themselves as Christians.

I read somewhere of a fond mother who was disappointed in her only daughter's choice of a husband; the girl had not selected the "right" son-in-law. He just wouldn't do.

And then the disappointed mother-in-law got a bright idea. She was a profoundly religious woman. She believed in prayer and she decided to make the young husband over! By prayer. Daily she prayed that he might become the man she had hoped her daughter would marry. Presently that prayer was answered. He became! Doubtless she became, too, but at any rate, that woman now has the finest son-in-law in the world. She boasts of it. Long ago, teaching His disciples on the mountain, Jesus presented the formula for forgiveness. It worked again, as it always does, in the fond mother's case.

And it has worked for me. One Wednesday at noon I spoke at a pre-Easter service in a downtown theater in Schenectady, New York. My subject was Reconciliation. As I spoke, two men came and stood directly in front of me. They were not really there, not in flesh and blood, and the rest of my listeners could not see them, but for me they were there and they remained until I finished speaking. Then they went with me to my hotel room. They were men who had been very close to me and from whom I was now estranged. As I sat alone that afternoon, I again went carefully through all the circumstances that had led to our falling-out.

Again I won the debate. I had been right. They were mistaken and wrong. That settled it...only it didn't. And presently I realized that winning the debate was definitely not a victory, for I had lost my friends. Being right in my own mind was not enough.

I interrupted an important writing program that afternoon and all but missed a deadline the next day. But that afternoon of reflection led to one of the most important decisions of my life. A telegram went to New York City and a letter went West. I said essentially the same thing in each: "I want things to be again as they were before. And before Easter I come to you to ask forgiveness for anything that I have done, or anything you may think I have done that was not fair and right." That was about all. It was hard to think about doing it, but when I actually brought myself to do it, it was *very* easy. And then? A reply telegram came from New York and presently a letter came from the West. Each conveyed a message that misted my eyes and broke my heart but to heal it. "No, Dan" the telegram said, "I was wrong and I have been hungry for the old days. Let's get together very soon." We did, and it was almost as it had been before, but with something added.

One morning in another city, I opened the local paper to read that one of these old friends had died the night before—that they had found him lying as though asleep. How thankful and glad I was that I had sent the wire—that I had put the teaching of Jesus to use at a moment in my life when His help was most needed.

An enemy is a dead weight on your life. Even if a man thinks of himself as your enemy, you need have no enemy. Generally, the prayer that changes you changes your enemy. Prayer not only changes "things"; it changes people. You cannot *have* an enemy if you refuse to *be* an enemy.

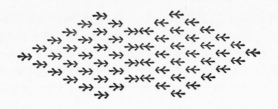

7. THE PEACEMAKERS

JESUS SAYS: *Blessed are the peacemakers: for they shall be called the children of God.*

MATTHEW 5:9

These words appear in what is generally acknowledged the greatest sermon ever preached, the sermon of the Beatitudes. Jesus stood upon a little mountain that looks down into blue Galilee and spoke to a multitude that hastily came out to Him from the surrounding towns and small cities.

The most unforgettable prayer meeting I ever attended fixed these words in my soul forever. It was held in a war blackout in front of Tebessa on the Gafsa Road in the spring of 1943. With Chaplain Colonel Roy Parker, then General Eisenhower's senior chaplain in North Africa and later Chief of Chaplains in the Army of the United States, I had come from Algiers to visit the Army's First Division. These were the days immediately preceding the Sicily campaign and after Rommel's advance through the Kasserine Pass had been stopped.

The regimental chaplain had his headquarters in a camouflaged, battered adobe house—hardly better than a hut. It was his custom after mess to have the men who were free and cared to come meet him for "family prayers." On this particular night the bombing was quite heavy; the enemy still had aerial superiority and took full advantage of it. But nine men came through the blackout and the moonless night to pray. They placed their tommy guns carefully on the dirt floor and sat on their helmets, backs against the wall. The chaplain opened with a brief prayer and then said: "The sergeant will read the evening lesson." And the sergeant, a young Vermonter who had enlisted on the day of Pearl Harbor, read the first nine verses of the fifth chapter of the Gospel of St. Matthew. His voice was low and quiet, but it carries across all the miles and years between that adobe hut and the room in which I now sit and write. Never shall I forget the boy who read that night and what he read: "And seeing the multitudes, he went up into the mountain: and when he was set ... he opened his mouth, and taught them, saying, Blessed are the poor in spirit: for theirs is the kingdom of heaven."

He went on through those immortal verses until he came to the ninth. That verse he read twice. "Blessed are the peacemakers: for they shall be called the children of God." After the second reading he hesitated and then said quietly: "I think that is a good place to stop."

The chaplain asked me to close the brief and informal but nonetheless stirring service with a prayer, and then we went out into the night, stopping when challenged and coming to our nearby billets for our often-interrupted rest.

"Blessed are the peacemakers. . . ." It was not as a killer but as a peacemaker that the sergeant saw himself and his comrades that dark night on the violent Gafsa front. And it is as peacemakers that I remember them and shall always remember them. They did not make the war. They wished to have no part in it. But they were in it regardless.

The sergeant died in the morning under the bombs that scored hits on our hastily opened advance airbase. I saw his body lying in the first-aid tent just off the field. But I did not see *him;* he was not there. He had a rendezvous with God. In him the Scriptures were fulfilled. Blessed are the peacemakers, for they shall see God.

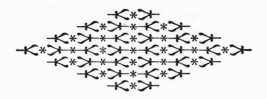

8. HOW JESUS GIVES

JESUS SAYS: ... *not as the world giveth,*
give I unto you.
JOHN 14:27

These words were spoken to the disciples following the Last
Supper. One of the most inspired and inspiring names given to
Jesus is "the Great Physician." Because our bodies are so
vividly apparent, so consciously a bane or a blessing, He is most
attractive, most appealing as the healer. But let us not make the
mistake of scorning the fruits of present-day medical research
and scientific discovery, for to reject the surgeon's skill and
the physician's knowledge is in effect to spurn Christ's healing.
Some things, many things, that Jesus did by Galilee He does
not need to do now. He counts on us. For example, in any
faith clinic for the relief of physical pain and for spiritual
healing there should be physicians and dentists, nurses and
social-service workers, dietitians and motherly women, skilled
people and practical people. In such a program prayer will al-

ways have exceptional power with God, power reaching beyond any human skill or finite authority.

A man who had been terribly injured in an accident, whose life had been despaired of, and whose recovery had been marveled at by some brilliant doctors, said one morning while specialists were consulting above him, "Gentlemen, either your X rays were mistaken and your diagnosis was incorrect, or more than human surgery has been at work here." Meeting squarely the challenge in the patient's eyes, one of the physicians replied: "Right, and the X rays were not mistaken. The diagnosis was correct."

The prayer of faith does heal the sick. The prayer of faith is the most powerful thing in the world. It has a certain authority with both heaven and earth. It is a lifeline thrown about the rock of the infinite.

This seems to me to be the very heart of the message that Bethlehem angels declared as the "good tidings of great joy": healing for the sick, mercy for the oppressed, triumph for the discouraged, gladness for the sorrowful, food for the hungry, courage for the burden-broken, a new heart for the sinner, and a new life for the dead. And this was and is the heart of the Christian message: joy, hope, health, peace, mercy, food, courage, and life everlasting.

I have seen the face of a holy man of the East set toward the distant pagoda of his penitence, his body scarred by self-inflicted wounds, his form emaciated by starvation, his clothing a single filthy rag, his countenance lined by nameless woes. The man was a devotee. He had given all for his religion, and his religion had made him what he was—a spectacle of misery. His fidelity, the steadfastness of his quest no man might question; but how futile and appalling his approach!

I have seen such faces in the East, but as I write now, thinking of Christ's healing, it is not the eastern holy man's face I see; it is my mother's face. I see it again through the lenses of infancy, when it was so magnified that it covered my gaze. I see it in the morning of our final parting when her eyes smiled through her tears. I see it in the shadow of privation and anxiety and with the lines of grief running to and fro upon it, lines as deep as those that earlier marked her hands when they rested softly on a strangely silent cradle. I see my mother's face alight with the flames from an inner fire as she sings the sweetest songs I ever heard. I see it in the latter days with its crown of soft and shining light. And in that light I read again the message of the angel chorus, "good tidings of great joy"— the message that rose to its crescendo in sorrow and in sickness and by a silent cradle, the message that is implicit in the promise of Jesus, "not as the world giveth, give I unto you."

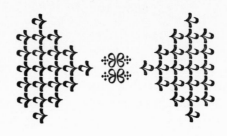

9. THOU FOOL!

JESUS SAYS: *Thou fool....*
LUKE 12:20

These hard words are taken from one of the best-known parables of Jesus, which begins, "The ground of a certain rich man brought forth plentifully...." The rich man soliloquizes, "Soul, thou hast much goods laid up for many years; take thine ease, eat, drink, and be merry." But the conclusion of the parable is "Thou fool, this night thy soul shall be required of thee: then whose shall these things be...?"

Emerson offered trenchant thought on modern man's attitude toward worldly goods: "'Tis pitiful the things by which we are rich or poor, a matter of coins and carpets, a little more or less of stone and wood and paint; like the naked Indians of whom one is proud in possession of a red feather or a glass bead and the rest miserable because of want of it."

But let us not make the wrong deduction. Jesus' final words

on this subject are significant: "So is he [a fool] that layeth up treasure for himself, and is not rich toward God." Jesus in none of His sayings condemned possessions, nor did He condemn those who by their frugality and labors had become rich. He Himself associated with the rich and successful of His time as well as with the poor. He had words of praise for the Roman officer who from his estate erected a synagogue for the Jews. It was the abuse of wealth and the misdirection of riches—it was selfishness—that the Great Teacher condemned.

One of the wise men of my personal friendship and of my public ministry was a cultured, talented, and wealthy gentleman who lived to be ninety-five. At the age of fifteen he was the organist of a New York church. He became executive vice-president of a great bank and was for many years president of the American Bible Society. He was generous with his talents and his funds. He never said to himself or to anyone else, "Take thine ease" or "Eat, drink, and be merry." Certainly he lived a personally rewarding life. He had special interests and projects, and he traveled widely. Above all, this man was "rich toward God" and he shared his success with the church he loved and with his less fortunate fellow humans.

Once we sat discussing his wealth. He said to me, "You see, all my money can buy for me personally is a little more room! When I sail to Europe I have a suite instead of a cabin. I may ride in a longer car and take a longer time in parking it." And he smiled. Such was his philosophy and such his practice.

His wife, who had been his constant companion, died many years before I knew him, but she never ceased to be his companion and always expectantly he was traveling to meet her, going forward to reunion. This man had "much goods," but he held them in a conscious stewardship. Also he did not allow the things he possessed, the "red feathers" and the "glass beads," to engage more than a small fraction of his time and attention. He lived a good life. With him first things were first, and he was "rich toward God." By following his example insofar as we are able to in our individual situations and relationships, we, too, may be rich toward God.

10. WIN OVER WORRY

Jesus says: ...*take no thought....*
MATTHEW 6:31

These three words appear in the sermon of the Beatitudes,
or the "Sermon on the Mount," from which we have already
quoted. They are found in the verse reading "Therefore take
no thought, saying, What shall we eat? or, What shall we
drink? or, Wherewithal shall we be clothed?" And in the
following verse is the reassurance: "...your heavenly Father
knoweth that ye have need of all these things." In other
words, as He so often stated, directly or indirectly, "Let not
your heart be troubled"; do not worry. The Psalmist states
it thus: "Fret not thyself because of evildoers...." Again the
meaning is clear and the admonition is specific. Do not worry.
It is not work that kills, it is worry. Work, and plenty of it,
is health-giving.

You can seldom put upon a man more honest, inspiring
work than he can carry. But worry is "rust upon the blade"—

27

so said Henry Ward Beecher. A certain clergyman kept an entire ship's company in mental turmoil during World War I, while his vessel went zigzagging through the torpedo zones, because he saw a periscope in every whitecap and an enemy rocket in every shooting star. He was convinced that his wife would never see him again, and eventually his companions on that ship wished he had never left her.

And what a worrier Thomas Carlyle is said to have been! A neighbor's chickens gave him great annoyance, the rooster particularly. Mr. Carlyle remonstrated with the owner of the bird, who insisted that the rooster seldom crowed more than twice in a night. "That's just it," Carlyle replied. "How I suffer waiting for him!" And do we not, all of us, suffer in waiting: waiting for trouble, sorrow, misfortune?

Since we are all bound to worry, what are we going to do about it? How may we hope to win over worry? A poet once offered this suggestion:

> Don't worry and fret, faint-hearted,
> The chances have just begun,
> For the best jobs haven't been started,
> The best work hasn't been done.

Assume an aggressive attitude; take the offensive against worry. And begin by asking yourself the question: "Am I doing my level best to merit relief from anxiety—or am I a moral loafer?" Remember always, God helps those who help themselves. You cannot win with worry. God helping, you can win over worry.

But how? Isaiah writes, "I will trust and not be afraid." And the philosopher Henry James said, "The sovereign balm for worry is religion." Here is the Psalmist's formula: "Trust in the Lord, and do good...." Or, as it appears later in this same Psalm, the thirty-seventh: "Rest in the Lord, and wait patiently...." That "rest in the Lord" means literally "be carefree, have no concern." Jesus said it even more concisely: "...take no thought...."

A father was carrying his little girl high upon his shoulders. Her cheeks were blooming, her eyes dancing, and her laughter was singing like the water of a brooklet over the pebbles of its course. "Careful! Careful!" called out a bystander with mock caution, and the small one shouted down, "I'm not afraid; he's my daddy!"

God is our Father, and, entrusting our lives to him, we are not to be afraid.

11. FEAR OF THE UNKNOWN

JESUS SAYS: *And ye shall know the truth, and the truth shall make you free.*

Knowledge is power. The world surrenders to men and women who know. Jesus told the Jews in the Temple that to know the truth was to be free. And to know Him is to be free of fear of the unknown, which is of all fears the most deadly.

In children and in primitive peoples the fear of the unknown may be studied with comparative ease. With adults and where society is more advanced, the study is more difficult. The child runs screaming from the thundercrash, hides from the lightning, because thunder and lightning are a mystery. We may not fear the unknown in the abstract, and yet who escapes the first rush of terror inspired by a typhoon or an earthquake? Perhaps our very knowledge may at times inspire fear.

When I was in college, our coach used to say, "Secret practice doesn't amount to much so far as you fellows are concerned, but it does keep your opponents on the griddle. So turn out!" It is the unknown that drives sweat to the contender's brow, whether he be an athlete, a soldier, an honest businessman, a parent waiting for a child after the approved hour of return, or a fleeing criminal. The fear of unknown, uncharted seas drove the crew of Columbus' ships to all but open rebellion. The human mind is an active agent. It must and will fill the unknown—if not with facts, then with phantoms. Plato wrote, "It is better to be unborn than to be untaught." The great teachers, the intrepid explorers, the indomitable scientists have been capturing and winning the knowledge that is setting us free of fear and ignorance.

Yet we continue to fear the future because the future is unknown. I once spent some weeks with a family whose members were in constant anxiety because death—the unknown—had never come to break their intimate circle. They were now apprehensive lest there would be that first break that would open the way for others in succession. There were aged members in that home and the spirit of the house was utterly demoralizing.

Even as we fear the future because of what it may hold for us, so we often fear ourselves, and here again because we do not know ourselves. Were you ever surprised by some sudden and insane rage, a seizure that left you trembling with horror at what you might have done? A father whose son had disobeyed him inexcusably seized an ax and hurled it at the boy's head. He missed his mark, but ever after he lived in fear, horrified by the thought that he had willed to kill his son. There are as yet undiscovered areas in our moral being.

How do we lose our fears of the unknown, of the future, of

ourselves—and even our fear of God, which for some is constant and at times little short of overwhelming? How? By following the formula of Jesus: "...ye shall know the truth, and the truth shall make you free." We lose our fear of God, as I long ago discovered, by "knowing Him" as He is. By knowing Him through the instruction of nature and the discoveries of science? Yes, all of these play their part and play it well, but they do not complete the matter. They fall far short of that. We know God at last and conquer our fear of death at last through Jesus Christ, in whom we find God fully revealed. We know Him as longsuffering and generous, sacrificial and kind. We know him as Savior and Lord, know Him as Jesus presents Him to us in what we call "The Lord's Prayer," as the omnipotent Father of us all: *"Our Father."*

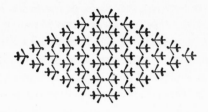

12. STONE-CASTERS STOPPED

JESUS SAYS: *He that is without sin among you, let him first cast a stone at her.*
JOHN 8:7

A bellowing mob came dragging an adulteress into the presence of the Great Teacher. There were others no doubt a hundredfold more guilty of lawbreaking than she. This does not excuse her sin or ease her condemnation, but from the beginning it is the woman who has been dragged into the pitiless glare of pharisaical publicity.

These men came reveling in the woman's disgrace and happy in the chance to drag it into the light. Jesus knew them for what they were. With a gesture of silence that said more plainly than any spoken word, "I understand; you do not deceive me," He stooped and with His finger traced in the sand. Then He faced them, and with eyes that stripped them to their moral nakedness, He said, "He that is without sin among you, let him first cast a stone at her." What followed was a precipitous retreat.

33

Jesus gave no clearance for sin or evil that day. He was deal-
ing, rather, with hypocrisy and malice. He stood to save and
not to judge, to give life and not to take it. He knew both
the motives of the would-be destroyers and the deepest
thoughts and desires of the hapless victim when He said,
"Neither do I condemn thee: go, and sin no more."

Must it be always stones only for others? Sometimes I think
that the faults in others that I most resent are those closest
akin to my own pet delinquencies. Perhaps I resent com-
petition.

> The faults of our neighbors with freedom we blame,
> Though tax not ourselves when we practice the same.

No stones were cast that day because there were no hands
to hold them and no arms to hurl them. It has been said that
"he shall be immortal who liveth until he be stoned by one
without fault." True enough. Conscience-smitten, the mob
melted away. "Conscience is a thousand swords," wrote
Shakespeare, and another wise man declared that conscience
is "God's deputy in the soul."

Never have I found Jesus more clearly and characteristically
supreme over the spiritual forces of the universe than when
He faces that stone-ready mob and with flashing eye says,
"He that is without sin among you, let him first cast a stone
at her." Notice that these words are not a refusal but an
invitation. And yet those fifteen words sent men stripped and
naked of soul down from the tribune of judgment into the ashes
not of His condemnation but of their own.

There is still another reason why there were no stones cast
that day. The stones were there, the criminal was there, the
mob was there—but Jesus was there. It was a good thing for

the woman that Jesus was there. And a good thing for all of us, for you and for me. A good thing for us it is that when vengeance would strike and when temptation moves in to overwhelm us, *He is there!* At such a moment, even though a crowd of the violent or the markedly unfriendly may surround us, we have the strength and courage to meet our ordeal, whatever that ordeal may be.

Of Stephen, the first martyr, who was dragged outside the walls of Jerusalem and stoned to death, it is written that he "cried with a loud voice, Lord, lay not this sin to their charge." No man stood with Stephen that day, but he was not alone. Abraham Lincoln, before the battle of Gettysburg, was alone—yet after he prayed he was not alone. Florence Nightingale was completely alone when she made her decision to go to the Crimean war front—and yet she testified that she was never alone. And in my own hours of uncertainty, whenever I have felt myself isolated and without human companionship, I have been comforted by the prayer of Jesus, "And yet I am not alone because the Father is with me."

13. THE FORBIDDEN PATH

JESUS SAYS: *Go not into the way of the Gentiles....*

MATTHEW 10:5

The message of Jesus and His healing ministry was first to His own people, the Jews. Indeed, at the beginning it was exclusively for the Jews. When He called His twelve disciples and, as Matthew tells us, "gave them power against unclean spirits,...and to heal all manner of sickness and all manner of disease," He commanded them, saying, "Go not into the way of the Gentiles...." But steadily His message and His ministry broadened until they became universal and were to all men and women and little children of all races and colors and conditions.

In 1950, I made my sixth visit to the Holy Land. There, Jesus captured my imagination, not only as the Lord and Savior of the Christian—my Lord and Savior—but as the inspired and glorious Jew. I write now as I found Him then.

It was on the Mount of the Beatitudes, high above blue

Galilee, that I attended a communion service. Representatives of nine Protestant denominations participated in this historic memorial—and nuns of the hostel on the Mount supplied the bread and wine, juice crushed from the native grapes and dark, heavy bread baked by devoted hands. There was an added touch when my friend, our Jewish guide, went with me to explain to the nuns our need of these communion emblems. He remained then to observe the simple feast.

A little later, I helped plant the last five of the first thirty thousand trees of the Children's Memorial Forest located at Ein Hashofet, the Louis Brandeis memorial village. It is our hope that eventually a million and a quarter trees, one tree for each child destroyed by Hitler, will cover the hills that look out upon the Vale of Esdraelon, hills that in 1935, when I first saw them, were barren as the sun-baked mesas of New Mexico.

As I stood by the last little tree, my Jewish friend pointed to my left and said, "There is the eastern end of the Carmel Range, just four miles or less from where we stand. The little building on the summit is a monastery that covers the traditional cave of Elijah where the ravens came. Yonder, less than twenty miles away, is Nazareth. That abrupt cliff is the spot from which they would cast Jesus down. Below us is the line of the old Roman road. There Jesus walked."

I queried, "But you don't believe all that?"

He smiled and replied, "Do you?"

"Yes," I said, "it is my tradition and my faith."

And then my friend took over the conversation. "But sir, there is something you do not understand," he said. *"Jesus is our boy!"*

There for me came a great awakening. Among the little

trees I saw this new Israel with a new light shining on it. This land so small includes everything of the Jew. Here are gathered together all the great ones, all the traditions, all the achievements, all the glories of Jewish history. No longer is the Jew a wanderer, a man without a country. Israel with even the vast southern Negev added may be scarcely as large as Vermont, but it includes everything from Ur of the Chaldees until the present; and it is a nation as great as human history.

That day at the Children's Memorial Forest, my Jewish friend stood with dignity like an ancient king of his people. I saw him and his fellow Israelis as the inheritors of the past even as they are the builders of the present. Abraham and Isaac, Moses and Isaiah, the shepherd king and the prophets, Deborah and the Maccabees and Jesus all belong to them.

"Jesus is our boy," my friend said and went on. "I have conducted perhaps five hundred parties of Christians through Israel, but until I observed your holy meal on the Mount of the Beatitudes I had never seen a Christian in an observance of his faith. That moved me deeply, and I say to you now that it means something to me to realize that hundreds of millions of Christians in the world worship our boy."

Many years ago, I heard the great Jewish rabbi Dr. Stephen Wise say in a lecture before the student body of my Christian college in Oregon, "Jesus! Jesus! of my own people, whom I love and honor, whom you worship and serve." And so it is that Jesus, however men may acclaim Him, cannot be escaped. Historically He is universal. And from that first "Go ye not into the way of the Gentiles," the healing ministry, the saving grace of Jesus Christ has become universal in the universal promise and invitation of Jesus Himself: "Whosoever will, may come."

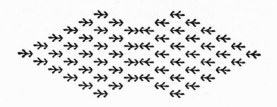

14. PERSONAL LIBERTY

JESUS SAYS: *Thou shalt love thy neighbor as thyself.*   MATTHEW 19:19

These words were among those spoken by Jesus to the rich young man who came to Him with the question, "Good Master, what good thing shall I do, that I may have eternal life?" The answer of Jesus has far-reaching social significance. Many years ago a wise man said in my presence, "Your personal liberty ends where your neighbor's nose begins." Liberty, when it is selfish, when it is without love, is always a dangerous thing. And all the freedom of thought and action that we as individuals possess is ours because men and women have from time to time surrendered their personal liberties in the interest of public welfare. No one has or could have unrestrained independence in any community where other men and women are without injury to his neighbors and therefore injury to himself, for by breaking down customs and laws agreed upon to protect all he would help remove his own safeguards.

Let us return to the homely saying, "Your personal liberty ends where your neighbor's nose begins." I have every right to swing my arms vigorously—a perfect right. But if another man is within an arm's length of me and I swing heedlessly, vigorously, or angrily, there may be and very likely will be something of a riot. Canadian thistles are beautiful when in their purple bloom, but you may not grow them in your yard. The thistledown with seeds for many thistles would be carried by the autumn winds into your neighbors' yards, and thistles are very properly regarded by society as a pest. You have a right to walk freely the streets of your city and to appear unmolested in any public place—until you contract measles or some other infectious disease, and then a very practical "love" of your neighbors keeps you at home. A man must not drive his car without regard; one poorly or selfishly managed automobile often congests a crowded street for many minutes. You may not even eat at your will. If you believe otherwise, remember that even in our eating the future builds upon the present. Today, sanatoriums, clinics, and rest homes are crowded with dyspeptics who were the gourmandizers of yesterday. Why do we regard one who tries to take his own life as a lawbreaker? Why may he even be imprisoned if he survives the attempt? Because the effect upon society is bad, leading others who may be neurotic to regard their lives lightly, setting a poor example to youth, and exerting an evil influence on the entire community.

There can be no peace in the home, no profit in business, no justice in government, no safety in society, no happiness, no abiding culture, no security for anyone without sincere consideration of others—their comfort, their health, their rights, their over-all well-being. This "love" that Jesus commended to the rich young man who came to Him was at once a very practical and powerful thing. He has most who gives most and he is most beloved who most loves.

Following World War II an English mother received a letter from a young German who had participated in the attack during which her son was killed. The German had been with the boy when he died. Both were wounded, and, forgetting the brutal conflict that had made them enemies, they comforted one another. With his last strength the English youth gave his wallet, with his mother's picture, to the German and said, "Send it back to her if ever there is the chance, and tell her how we were together here." There is more to the story, but this is its blessed ending: The mother in England reached out in the spirit of love that Jesus advocated and into her arms and heart drew the homeless German soldier who had given her son his mortal wound.

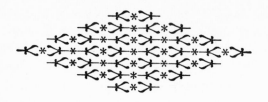

15. THE MIDNIGHT VISITOR

JESUS SAYS: *Ye must be born again.*

JOHN 3:7

Nicodemus, who was a Pharisee and a man of distinction among the Jews, came to Jesus in the night and between them occurred a conversation that is one of the most profound in all the annals of metaphysical writing. When, in reply to the courteous salutation of His visitor, Jesus said, "...Except a man be born again, he cannot see the kingdom of God," Nicodemus replied, "How can a man be born when he is old?" The Master answered that it was the spiritual rebirth of which He spoke: "That which is born of the flesh is flesh: and that which is born of the Spirit is spirit." Jesus then went on to compare the spiritual new birth to the wind which "...bloweth where it listeth, and thou hearest the sound thereof, but canst not tell whence it cometh...." And when Nicodemus demurred and said "How can these things be?" the Master chided him with, "Art thou a master of Israel, and knowest not these things?" The amazing conversation continued, and in it appear what are perhaps the best-known of all the words of Jesus: "For God so loved the world, that he gave his only begotten Son, that whosoever believeth in him should not perish, but have everlasting life."

Are we not impressed by the fact that Jesus received His after-hours visitor courteously on his own recognition and knew him for what he was—an honest though perhaps timid seeker after truth? I wonder what would have happened had Nicodemus been curtly answered and summarily dismissed; had the Great Teacher said in effect, "My office hours are eight to three, sir. Call my secretary and make an appointment." Well, I imagine that Nicodemus, crestfallen, chagrined, and perhaps embittered, would have gone his way. He would have lost the "unspeakable gift." He would have lost the vital answer he received, and we would have lost it too! We would have lost some of the most eloquent words and exquisite sentences of the human language. Nor would there have been a masterful voice raised in protest when later on the officers and chief priests cursed and condemned Jesus. How deep an impression was made in that interview of Nicodemus with Jesus we shall never know, but we do know that it was an abiding impression, for he was one of two men who, having had during His lifetime no open relations with the Nazarene, stepped forward boldly at His death and bore His body to its burial. Never again are these two men mentioned in the Holy Scriptures, but we remember them with a grateful, wistful tenderness. And we like to believe that in all the spiritual reality of that blessed event Nicodemus was "born again."

One thing yet remains to be written of that midnight conversation. The great question is not "when does a man come to Jesus?" or even "How does a man come to Jesus?" The great question is "How does he go away from his interview, and when he goes what does he carry with him?"

I have a friend in New York who, in the decade before we met, lost just about everything that makes life worth living— family, friends, a gainful position, and self-respect. Then he went to Jesus—went literally in the night as well as in the darkness of his despair. And that last darkness was so dense that he had decided to throw his body into the river; he felt it was not worth saving. But before he went to the river's edge, he flung himself down in the old Bowery Mission. He tells us now that he heard Jesus say "Ye must be born again," and in his despair he did not turn away "sorrowful" as Nicodemus did from his first meeting with Jesus. My friend claimed then and there the promise "ask and ye shall receive" and he was "born again." The mystery of the New Birth became real in this man. Today, his wife and children are with him again, and after six years of this experience he is still "the new man in Christ Jesus" with a new and radiant life of joy and service.

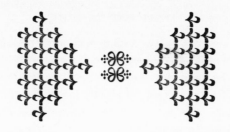

16. PRAYER AND PHYSICAL HEALING

JESUS SAYS: *They that are whole need not a physician; but they that are sick.*

LUKE 5:31

Jesus had gone for dinner with Levi, a publican, and publicans were unacceptable to the churchmen of His time. They criticized Him and His desciples. "Why do you eat with sinners?" the critics demanded, and He replied, "They that are whole need not a physician; but they that are sick."

Always in illness I have sent others to, and have given myself to, competent medical practitioners. I believe that God and His Son, the Great Physician, would have us use the skills and the discoveries that man's mind and ever-searching spirit have found for our well-being. My own ministry has been immeasurably rewarded by my relationships and intimate friendships with doctors, nurses, and other scientifically trained healers.

The promise in James, that "the prayer of faith shall save the sick," has often been made the excuse and occasion of

45

charlatans and other designing people. Perhaps because of these abuses that have crept in, the Church, the Protestant Church particularly, in recent times has neglected the healing ministry that had so large and honorable a place in the early Church. There is no excuse for this neglect and happily there are increasing signs that the churches generally are returning to that promise.

The growth of Christian Science, Unity, and other similar groups is confirmation of the greater fact that "the Great Physician still is nigh," that Jesus Christ Who healed in Judea and Galilee heals here and now, that God is not baffled by even our "incurables," but is "the same yesterday, today, and forever." And the ministry of the Christian Church is forming partnerships with the medical profession and with science to bring comfort and recovery to those who are physically and mentally ill.

Only a few times in my own ministry have I been impelled to appeal in prayer for an abrupt decision in a sickness, and then only when there was an irresistible "leading."

Once in Canton, Ohio, I went to a home of great poverty. A little boy lay unconscious with pneumonia. Crying out with every breath, he seemed to be dying. The doctor had done everything he could and had gone away. The young mother cried out to me as the father held her and tried to comfort her. It was the second year of my ministry, but I felt as I had never felt before that prayer would save the sick. With my hand upon that fairly steaming brow, I prayed. The boy seemed to grow better immediately! And he lived.

That recovery was presently an embarrassment. The incident became a series of "recoveries" as it was told and retold in the community. I was in danger of being regarded as a professional faith healer, a practicing specialist. And never was I that. Indeed I never was "led" to be that. Mary, the mother of Jesus, said to His disciples at the marriage in Cana of Galilee, "Whatsoever he saith unto thee, do it." And that has been the word I have always waited for.

I do not question many other sincere and more competent operators in this vast field of needy men and women. *Rather, I envy them*. But save only in a very limited way, the healing authority has never been granted me. Perhaps God has had other things for me to do.

On two occasions when my wife was desperately ill, I have known that God was ready to release healing power through me. In each instance we were on a transcontinental train, the need was immediate and imperative, and "no other help was nigh." Once the crisis came between Portland and Klamath Falls in Oregon; once as we traveled between Pocatello, Idaho, and Cheyenne, Wyoming. Each time her excruciating pain was relieved under my hand, as I prayed. Each time the recovery was complete and the indications of conditions requiring a major surgical operation disappeared. "They that are whole need not a physician; but they that are sick." And in our extremity, when other doctors could not be summoned, "the Great Physician" Himself was on call.

17. NARROW ESCAPES

JESUS SAYS: *No prophet is accepted in his own country.*
LUKE 4:24

There are times when actions speak louder than words. In the life of Jesus such a time came when He angered the congregation in the synagogue of Nazareth. This was His home town, He was the son of Joseph, the local carpenter, and the townsmen were prejudiced against Him. With angry shouts they refused longer to listen to His condemning words. Forcing Him from the sanctuary, they hurried Him to the high cliff that drops abruptly to the plain leading to Jerusalem. Their purpose was to end His life then and there. But without a word He quietly turned, walked right through them, left them standing silenced and defeated. By human tests, it was a narrow escape.

For all of us, life is full of such escapes. In earlier times, simple-minded mothers (or were they so simple-minded?) were sure that for every child born, God set a guardian angel, else how could any baby survive and live to maturity? Today, we need to balance the zeal and ambition, the reckless hurry that the average healthy American has in such abundance, with the principle of "safety first." Less haste at the crossings would save us time in the hospitals. A timely vacation may forestall a fatal stitch in the chest. And a fool with his money is no more a fool than I am if I use my body for a garbage can and my mind for a cesspool.

But when these things are said, there remains the question, "Is escape always to be sought?" Jesus did not need an escape when He came to the great occasion of His life. I am not altogether and in every sort of a situation a disciple of "safety first." Certainly Jesus was not. Carry that too far and nothing gets done. Imagine Abraham, or Moses, or Stephen, or Paul, or Jesus; Arnold von Winkelried, the Pilgrims, George Washington, Abraham Lincoln, or the Christian missionaries organizing "safety first" clubs! And yet, in a sense and for their generations, that is exactly what they did do. They were adventurers and pathfinders, but they sought those sure foundations where freedom and righteousness and peace would at last be secure, and in their search they risked all.

The narrowest escapes of all are not physical. They are moral—the escape of Paul over the wall of Damascus. And how narrow an escape a man has when he finally eludes selfishness! Henry Ward Beecher once said that selfishness was a detestable vice which no one would ever forgive in others and which no one was without in himself.

But how are we to escape? How are we to escape physical destruction on streets and highways where drivers mix alcohol with gasoline? How are we to escape moral shipwreck on the high seas of twentieth-century society? And how is our very freedom—which we believe to be our unique and priceless way of life—to escape her foes within and without? I know of no answer to these questions that ignores the plain implications of the warning "How shall we escape, if we neglect so great a salvation?" Neglect itself is a surly sin and a fatal defect. Our sons cross the oceans to fight for our freedom, but too many of their fathers neglect to cross the street to vote for it. Men neglect their homes for business or golf, skimp their families and friends for the advancement that is often a retreat from happiness. Neglect is man's supreme spiritual failure—neglect, not repudiation, neglect, not denial. Neglect is indifference and indifference is as dry rot within the body and soul of American freedom. If liberty itself dies, it will die not at the hands of an invading foe but from neglect within. Jesus escaped by the sheer weight of His moral and spiritual authority, without speaking a word. And we shall escape from our social, economic, political, and spiritual dangers *if we do not neglect.*

Years ago, in a New Hampshire election when, during my absence in Europe, my neighbors named me as their candidate for the state legislature, I was first elected but in the recount defeated by *one* vote. And I knew of three voters in particular who were for me but had not troubled to cast their ballots.

18. FIGHT THE FALSE

JESUS SAYS: *Nay, lest while ye gather up the tares, ye root up also the wheat with them.*

MATTHEW 13:29

In the parable of the tares, Jesus advocated postponing their fate, not to show the tares consideration but to avoid the possible destruction of valuable grain. There is a wheat, or was in His time, that is so much like a poison weed until it is fully grown that it is almost impossible to distinguish it from the true wheat. In such a case there may be only one way to fight the false: The good and the bad must mature together.

From the beginning the false and the true have existed side by side; in politics, in business, in friendship, in ourselves. Particularly does it exist in children. It is a mistake to use rough and unsympathetic methods with a child when, to the adult mind, there has been a violation of the adult code. A boy of five placed a nickel in a chewing gum machine instead of in the Sunday-school box. A misguided adult accused him of stealing. There is for children only a hairline difference between "imagination" and falsehood. Far better for us to assume that children do not really lie or steal and govern ourselves accordingly in our instruction and discipline.

On the other hand, we invite disaster for the best and holiest things of life and for freedom itself when we cease fighting the false just because the false and the true exist side by side. As to practical details of the struggle, perhaps we can do vastly more for a worthy cause and for truth itself by living the good and true life than in any other way. We all have more need of models than of critics, and who does not judge a plan or a situation more definitely by the eye than by the ear, by what we do and are rather than by what we say we are? Christ, who never wrote a tract, a leaflet, or a book, went about doing good and so the world cannot forget Him.

Life's plan of battle is not always the same. There are direct attacks and frequently there are even more effective delayed and indirect attacks. There were times when Jesus moved with abruptness, as when He drove the moneychangers from the temple. There were times when He spoke in parables and when He even seemed to hesitate, but in every case He was making progress toward His objective. Actually, there was never a time in His incomparable life when He was not registering His influence against falsehood. There is always upon us the obligation to strike out against the false, to go on record as opposed to that which our minds elect as wrong. But we are not bound to win here and now, to rip out the tares at the risk of destroying the wheat. Jesus Himself lost the immediate battle. He was crucified, but He did not turn aside. He did not accept failure, and out of the disaster was shaped the triumph that has changed the world of human thought and action.

The fight with the false is a finish fight. Life's most pathetic figure is not the loser but the quitter, the physical or moral contender who does not run out his race but settles for inaction or silence. There may be cheers for the defeated runner who comes on through the crowd that swarms over the track behind the winner, but there will be none for the fellow who slows down on the backstretch and slinks off. Edward the Black Prince fought his greatest battle, won his finest victory with a hemorrhage on his lips but with a sword in his hand.

Victory we may not see—indeed we may fail in the particular event—but if we go through to the end, no matter how bitter it may be, we shall have done our best, and nothing else matters. During my boyhood my father identified himself with the conservation movement headed by Theodore Roosevelt and Gifford Pinchot. Conservation was then a controversial and highly unpopular cause in Oregon. Though never violently partisan, father lost some friends by standing quietly but firmly for what he regarded as best for the welfare of his state and country. When depleted forests elsewhere in America ultimately made the danger clear to all, father was vindicated and his friends looked upon him as a wise citizen who had not ceased working for the truth and the right.

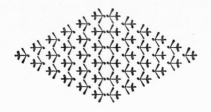

19. THE MOUNTAIN CLIMBER'S PERIL AND SAFETY

JESUS SAYS: *...he will guide you into all truth....*
JOHN 16:13

I am the way....
JOHN 14:6

Jesus made these statements, the first about His Father, the second about Himself, during His last conferences with His disciples. And He also said, "The Father and I are one." He was preparing them for the separation soon to come, for the tragic events leading to His betrayal and crucifixion. The men to whom He spoke had until then refused to believe His words, to accept the reality of His Kingdom, even though He had spoken of it clearly and often. Telling His disciples that His Kingdom was not of this world, and that He must die, He gave these two magnificent promises to men who had a rugged road ahead of them. Today, His promises are for all who would climb and win summits.

The perils of the climber are many, and many are unavoidable; others are avoidable but invite recklessness. Danger comes soonest when it is despised. Guides fear the careless members of a party far more than they fear the timid. Disobeying repeated warnings, an impetuous climber pressed out to the extreme front of an ice ledge. "Hey, look at me!" he shouted, and his companions watched in helpless horror as the place where he stood broke loose from the mountain and he went hurtling to his death.

No one climbing a mountain without a guide, up a trail to him unknown, can ever be sure of his safety. It is well to remind ourselves that "he only is safe from danger who remains on guard when he is safe" and that "danger frightens a timid person before it happens, a coward when it happens, and a hero after it happens." But the guide who knows that even a shrill cry may start an avalanche and who waves a warning to the careless fellow behind him—that guide is certainly not the coward of the party.

And in ordeals of every sort, whether they be physical or moral, the climber must have determination and be able to make decisions. A friend of mine became ill while ascending a mountain. He insisted on dropping out of the party rather than hold it back. This man was able to make a wise decision just as truly as another friend who, when the final test came, though he was dizzy and half blind, crawled inch by inch up the rope the last five hundred feet to the mountaintop.

With a single exception, the climber's safety is in himself. In his willingness to act quickly and decisively lies security for himself and for the entire party. If in a crisis he loses his nerve, if he fails of a fighting spirit, the plan of campaign must be revised and frequently the ascent must be abandoned.

The rarest foods and fruits may come to those who have not soiled their hands or clothes to possess them, but the summit of a mountain never comes to any man who does not take it for himself. Destiny is not a word, it is a work.

I have noted that with a single exception the climber's safety is in himself. That exception is the guide. I may have the stamina of a marathon runner, the strength of a modern Hercules, and the intuitions of a boy born in the Alps, but if I take the trail to unknown heights alone, I walk with death. Take a guide in your climb to the heights. Are you climbing, battling alone, today? Struggling, forging forward inch by inch, or losing ground against doubt and grief and frustration—alone? Take the Guide who says "I am the way"—and that way you will be guided "into all truth."

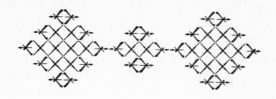

20. THE HIDDEN WORKERS

JESUS SAYS: *Whence shall we buy bread, that these may eat?*
JOHN 6:5

This question Jesus asked as He faced a "great multitude" on a small mountain above Lake Galilee. The people had come from all the surrounding country, drawn by His words and miracles. Now it was late and Jesus knew they were hungry. It is written that when He asked the question "he himself knew what he would do." Then it was that He took "five barley loaves, and two small fishes" and multiplied them so that He not only fed the thousands but had the disciples gather together the fragments until they filled twelve baskets.

All about us now, everywhere and in all things, there are the unnamed, hidden workers, men and women, who feed and clothe and house us. Their influence is in every stone and timber of our great buildings. They carry us in travel by land and sea and in the air. We may never see them, and be unconscious of them—until they fail—but they are ever with us.

My desk light flickers and burns low. Then I may think of the engineers I have never seen who listen day and night with practiced ear to the singing dynamos. I remember a summer when for days and weeks fresh milk appeared on my table and I gave it no real thought. Then one morning the pitcher was empty. The man who toiled in the night while I slept, who came to my door just as I yawned and turned over for my morning "finale," was suddenly taken sick. I had never counted him until he was counted out.

One midnight the Golden State Limited ground to an emergency stop a hundred miles north of El Paso, Texas, and my head crashed into the partition between the berths. Ever since, I have considered the astronomers to be conservative when they number the stars of the Milky Way by millions! That night a Mexican track-walker stood between us and death. His wildly swinging lantern stopped our engine at the brink of a gorge spanned only by charred and crumbling timbers. I never saw that track-walker. He had gone his way before most of us learned of his service. In gratitude, we left a purse for this hidden worker.

Christ built His Kingdom—and is building it today—with hidden workers, building it not upon the high priests of the Temple, but upon Peter the Fisherman of Galilee, and upon all those noble men and women who, at home or overseas, have organized churches and erected hospitals and schools and who have done all and suffered much without thought of acclaim or of personal reward. Certainly these largely nameless workers have their reward of joy and satisfaction, but it is not amiss for us to make up the purse and add the crown of our recognition with our heartfelt "thank you." The worker is worthy of his hire and of something added. Tradition tells us that the lad whose loaves and fishes gave Jesus a great opportunity that day became a follower of the Galilean and a leader in His cause. He had his great reward.

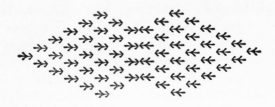

21. THE STRENGTH OF YOUTH

JESUS SAYS: *When a strong man armed keepeth his palace, his goods are in peace....*

LUKE 11:21

This militant verse appears in the same chapter with the prayer given by Jesus to His disciples, which begins "Our Father." But immediately following the verse appears this warning from the great and wise Teacher: "But when a stronger than he shall come upon him, and overcome him, he taketh from him all his armour wherein he trusted, and divideth his spoils." Jesus was pointing out the real source of strength, and doing so in the face of His critics and enemies. He had been accused of calling upon the powers of darkness to perform His wonders, but He claimed again for His ministry spiritual power, the power of God, Himself.

Youth learns a brave lesson from Jesus when it discovers the Master's attitude toward strength and its source. History reveals two attitudes toward weakness. The pagans cast their physically unfit to hungry beasts or exposed them to life-destroying weathers. In our time, Hitler employed a similar program against millions who were too weak to resist him. Christian civilization, on the other hand, builds hospitals, clinics, asylums, schools. The indication of the kindlier attitude in human strength is found in contributions made to society by a Charles Proteus Steinmetz or a Booker T. Washington. The one, with a twisted body and a hump between his shoulders, harnessed the infinite powers of electricity with hitherto undreamed-of discoveries, and the other rose from slavery to become a Moses of his race. But always, as there must be sound metal to make sound chain, such as these must have a sound character and be spiritually fine.

Youth needs such examples in every generation, needs, too, the lesson that metal, however sound, must be tempered and shaped to make it into a sound finished product. The most brilliant athlete I ever knew lost his chance for a place on an Olympic team because he deliberately broke training rules and wrecked his splendid body. Dissipation came and took his proud armor.

Moral preparation is even more essential than physical. We oldsters may know now how important it is to keep the fine edge that was first sharpened in our eager and less sophisticated youth.

Spiritual preparation is a further step ahead, for by it we prepare to keep in stride with God, to walk the friendly, conquering way with another young man—Jesus of Nazareth.

Be sure of one thing, young man, young woman: whether prepared or not, armed or unarmed, you will be tested—your body, your mind, and your heart. Some years ago a lad of seventeen was the only entrant to finish in the grueling race from the mainland of California to Catalina. He must have had a well-nigh perfect body. His swimming form for that test could hardly have been less than perfect. But beyond that his was a sturdy, marching soul—and so he won.

There is always for youth a greater race than that to Catalina to enter and win. And always the armor that Jesus talked about, the armor of both the body and soul, is vital to success. Always, too, the incomparable Youth of Nazareth who conquered seas of passion and despair, even as He calmed Galilee, is ready and eager to show the way and inspire the deed.

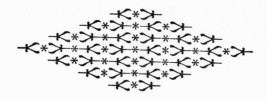

22. THE COURAGE OF KNOWLEDGE

JESUS SAYS: *I . . . know my sheep, and am known of mine.*
JOHN 10:14

There were times, many times, when Jesus had to repeat Himself to be understood, when even His disciples were uncertain of His meaning. But He never left them in uncertainty. He would repeat and rephrase, as in this instance when a parable of the sheepfold was "understood not." Then it was that Jesus said and repeated, "I am the good shepherd, and know my sheep, and am known of mine." As to Jesus Himself, it is impossible to define, to explain Him, even adequately to describe Him. There were many names given Him—Shepherd, Door, Prince of Peace, Lamb of God, Great Physician, Light of the World, and still others; yet, as Emerson said, "When we attempt to describe Him both language and thought desert us and we are as helpless as fools and savages." But we may *know* Him, Whom we cannot describe. And the sort of knowledge that we have of God, or may come to have through Jesus Christ, in Whom He is fully and convincingly revealed, gives us courage. This sort of knowledge is power.

But this knowledge must be paid for since, as the Bible says, we must study to show ourselves approved. It takes training, long training, to become an expert marksman. You cannot bluff through a real crisis in your life. Everywhere and always we face the fact that our learning days are never over. A false pride is frequently a handicap, for it suggests to those who lack information that it is a confession of weakness to ask questions. An Eastern philosopher, on being asked how he had acquired his scholarship, replied that it was by not being prevented by shame from seeking information when he was ignorant.

One afternoon in New York City I walked into Gramercy Park, walked in like a lord and out somewhat like a thief when a guard informed me that the park was a private preserve. I would have avoided embarrassment had I asked before I followed another visitor through the open gate. I did not become wise about the rules till too late.

Knowledge of God may be sought and will always be found. An experience in the first year of my ministry remains with me, as vivid now as it was on the day it occurred. For an hour I waited by the bed of a dying woman, the mother of six children. They were all gathered there, the eldest a girl of fifteen, the youngest a tiny baby, and the grief-stricken father. Never since that hour have I known a more tragic pastoral ordeal. In my extremity I cried out and God heard me—but the voice in which He spoke was the voice of the dying woman. With her head upon the pillow that was like an island in a sea of tears, and with her toilworn hands pressing against her heart the youngest of the six, she held me with her smile and said, "I know Him whom I have believed, and am persuaded that He will keep that which I have committed unto Him against that day." She went on then in a faltering voice, "The Lord is my shepherd...." And before she asked me to pray she whispered to her husband, "He relieveth the fatherless and the widows, John, and I know that He will care for you and the motherless." She died then in high courage, the courage of her perfect knowledge, knowledge of the Shepherd who knew and received her.

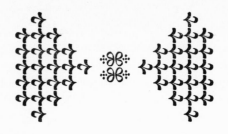

23. TRAILS TO THE HEARTS OF MEN

JESUS SAYS: *Settle it therefore in your hearts....*

LUKE 21:14

Jesus spoke to the minds of men always, but always He sought to win and hold their hearts. The words "settle it therefore in your hearts ..." stand in the midst of His prophecy of the destruction of the Temple at Jerusalem and His commendation of the gift of the poor widow who gave her two mites, the smallest of coins, while rich men in scorn of her cast their wealth into the treasury.

To belittle the heart has always been a favorite diversion of a certain class of "intellectuals." Those who have pride of mind, based upon superficial intellectual equipment, appear to despise the show of emotion. This, of course, is not right. The mind creates the plan of vast proportions, but without the heart the plan fails of becoming a practice. The mind may be the transportation system, but the heart is the dynamo. It was the heart of Abraham Lincoln finally, and not his intellect, that made him the greatest and at the same time most human figure in the world of statesmanship.

There are four trails to the hearts of men, and Jesus knew and traveled them all. Fear is first. Fear which may be either vicious or virtuous; fear which may be the by-product of faith leading to hope, or fear which is the child of doubt crying out in despair. Not to fear when there is occasion for fear is as great a weakness as cowardice and may lead to a worse disaster. Fear may be a gong that brings the mind into quick life upon the approach of danger.

The second trail to the hearts of men is reason—reason which makes man different, which distinguishes him from the lower animals. Reason was one of Christ's direct paths to the hearts of men. There is never a conflict between reason and truth, though many of us offer reasons as excuses for rejecting truth. Reason and revelation are twins, and the absence of one dims and may destroy the light of the other. It has been said that "he who will not reason is a bigot, who cannot is a fool, and who does not is a slave," and Isaiah of Israel said, "Come let us reason together." The secret of reason's power lies in the fact that it wins all by compelling none.

But reason at last discovers only the continents that lie near at hand, knows nothing of all that lies beyond and above. Robert Ingersoll said, "If I go to Heaven, I want to take my reason with me." But already he had announced that his reason had failed to discover Heaven. Conscience, the deep inner voice of man's soul, is a surer trail to the hearts of men, because conscience is the voice of God in the soul. Also, conscience is the pulse of reason.

There remains one other way to the hearts of men, the way of love. This is peculiarly the ultimate, the divine way, because as Jesus Himself said, "God is love." Long ago a poet declared "Love reasons without reason." But better still, love reasons both with and beyond reason. Where reason despairs, love hopes on, where the mind muddles, love masters, where intellect doubts, love invokes faith, and love is always more just than justice. Love is comprehensive of all worthy emotions and the only royal road to the hearts of men. These, then, are the trails to the hearts of men—fear, reason, conscience, love. And the greatest of these is love.

One of the poignant illustrations of this way of love came to me many years ago, not from man but from beast. I was in a party hunting mountain lions in the Kaibab Forest on the north rim of the Grand Canyon. Suddenly and mysteriously our baying dogs fell silent. We soon came upon them; they stood motionless in a circle about a dying doe. Trained to track lions, not deer, they had followed the scent to the lion's victim. With her hindquarters helpless, the doe had raised herself upon her forelegs to face the hounds and us. Close against her stood a spotted fawn. That dying mother shook her head at us and with her last convulsive breath defended her young. Call it instinct if you choose, but it was the mother purpose and passion that in human beings we call love. And for me, that day, the doe's love just about dissolved my enthusiasm for all hunting.

24. CLAIM TODAY

JESUS SAYS: *This day is salvation come to this house....*
LUKE 19:9

Jesus spent a night with Zacchaeus, a rich and despised tax collector. Being a man of small stature, Zacchaeus had climbed into a tree that he might see Jesus as He passed, and Jesus, seeing him, called him down, saying to the surprise of everyone, "...today I must abide at thy house." And Zacchaeus, it is written, "made haste, and came down, and received him joyfully." The little publican claimed today and got himself not only a distinguished guest but salvation and peace of mind.

Today is, yesterday was, tomorrow never will be. Today is the only day you and I may claim. To live in the past is futile and to wait on tomorrow is at best a child's fancy, for when the dawn comes it is today.

There are a few misguided people who refuse to claim today because today is all they have. They will not cultivate flowers because flowers fade. They will not have pets be-

cause the life of a canary is five years or less and the life of
a dog may be no more than twelve years. They refuse to form
close friendships because death must inevitably separate friends.
They do not believe that it is better to have loved and lost than
never to have loved at all. And yet, these people do claim today
for they cannot escape it. But theirs is not its glory, but its
shadow; not its happiness, but its fears; not its beauty, only its
ashes.

Long ago, in Portland, Oregon, I met and came to know a
girl of unusually attractive face and spirit. The first time I felt
her hand in mine I was startled by its unnatural chill. With an
exclamation, I commented upon the fact. She laughed and
said, "Yes, and nothing can be done about it. I have been just
about everywhere and gone to everyone, but they tell me I am
doomed slowly to freeze to death." And again she laughed an
infectious, adorable laugh.

Singing, working, serving to the very last, she went on, in
her church and her youth group. Her city came to know and
love her. Then one day a friend wrote and told me of how
they had found her one morning on the cot on the sleeping
porch with her now-peaceful, once-radiant, vibrant face turned
toward Mount Hood, the view she loved more than any other.
"Helen must have suffered terribly at times, but no one ever
knew," my friend wrote. Helen claimed today. For her there
were no dark tomorrows and no painful yesterdays. She lived
and laughed and loved in the friendships and flowers and tasks
of the present.

Her life was a symphony, and a symphony is not an accident.
For her serene and victorious spirit there was a reason. She was
sufficient for her ordeal because when she claimed today she

claimed God, and in claiming Him her soul was a little corner of Heaven because her Heavenly Father lighted it.

But is today all we have? Is there no tomorrow? Yes, today is all we have, but it is enough, because we may discover, as Helen did, that today never ends. It is the morning of eternity and the dawn of our immortality.

25. THE LONGEST DISTANCE, THE SHORTEST WAY

JESUS SAYS: *Go, wash in the pool of Siloam....*

JOHN 9:7

In his miraculous healing of the man who had been blind from birth, the Great Physician took the long and not the short way. Jesus did not say directly, "Receive your sight. See!" He mixed the clay, anointed the eyes, and sent the man, who no doubt moved slowly and with some difficulty, to the pool. Then his faith and obedience rewarded the one who had been blind. He came seeing. For him the longest distance that day was the shortest way.

As a rule, haste makes waste. In time beauty is born, thoroughness is achieved, and in the forty years of Israel's wandering in the wilderness a great triumph was prepared for.

Some insects are born, live, and finish their course in less than an hour. By contrast, a dog that followed at my heels and tangled herself up with my heart lived beyond her time, though she died in her sixteenth year. But a man develops socially, intellectually, and spiritually through fifty, seventy, ninety, or even a hundred years only to discover that he is at the beginning of his immortality.

The miracles of Jesus further emphasize this principle of preparation and delay. He fed the five thousand. The power that multiplied the bread and increased the fishes could have willed the hungry satisfied, but He took the longer route. He bade them sit down upon the hillside. He sent the disciples forward with the food, and out they went again to gather up the fragments. And when the blind man's sight was restored, clay was first prepared as an ointment. We should not expect to reap a harvest as soon as we have planted the seed.

But despite the seeming delays, God's way is so short a man can understand and follow it. He leads us forward as rapidly as we are able to go. He brings us to our supreme moments as soon as we are ready. Israel did not get into Canaan one day too soon. God's way is the way of authority, the way marked out by a competent guide. There is another way, one which "seemeth good unto a man, but the end thereof are the ways of death."

The final test for any way is, "Does it arrive?" A young man traveling in northern New England for the first time came to a crossroad. There were no signs; the traveler asked a villager who came by which turn to take. The native pointed to the less attractive road. The traveler demurred, saying, "The other looks better to me." The villager answered laconically, "Yes, it looks good, but doesn't go there."

I hear the voice of final authority and of unrivaled wisdom saying, "I am the way. . . ." Be the road long or short, difficult or sometimes easy, His is the way through, the way out, the way to the destination we at our best and bravest desire to reach. The blind man, as of the record, did not question the direction he had been given, did not hesitate. He took the road pointed out and returned with his sight.

It is the conclusion of a great company of men and women who have gone forward facing the ordeals of life, making the difficult climbs, traversing the often barren distances, that Jesus is "the way," and that however long the journey, when it is with Him it is always the shortest way.

There have been times of crisis in my life when I have been undecided as to the course I should take, the decision I should make. At such moments I have said in my prayers, "Father, I have put everything I have into my search for the answer, and I am still undecided. But this seems now to be the road I should take. If it is the wrong road, stop me! Put a block across it!" This may be a dangerous prayer, but if we are to live abundantly, as Jesus calls upon us to live, we must live dangerously. And I have found the prayer effective: I have sometimes been directed to what seemed the longest road, but I have always arrived safely.

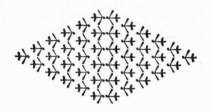

26. WHAT MAKES GOD GLAD

JESUS SAYS: *And if so be that he find it, verily I say unto you, he rejoiceth more of that sheep, than of the ninety and nine which went not astray.*

MATTHEW 18:13

With His parables of the lost sheep and the searching shepherd, the lost coin and the rejoicing woman, the returning prodigal and the welcoming father, Jesus makes forever clear the attitude of the Heavenly Father and His own attitude toward the wanderer and the outcast. And here, too, He gives us the reason for His tireless labors and the very business of His being, which is the saving of the frustrated and lost.

Jesus has presented us with the complete picture of the love of the Heavenly Father, a love all-powerful, all-discerning, and not conditioned upon our acknowledgment or even acceptance of it. Above every other attribute of the Infinite and Almighty One stands the stupendous fact that God loves man, loves him in his ignorance, loves him in his waywardness, loves him in his sin—loves him, as Mark Guy Pierce once said, "with a love that makes Him sad, but loves him." And of course God loves man when he is doing well, with a love that "makes Him glad."

God, as Jesus presented Him in these three parables, finds His supreme happiness not in creating worlds but in searching out lost children and in welcoming home prodigal sons and daughters. But why? Why does so infinitesimal a thing as a single prodigal's return, the recovery of one lost lamb among countless billions, make God glad? Because He is infinite and because the prodigal is always His son. Because if our Christian faith is justified, God has the same infinitely intimate relation to each and all that you have to your son and daughter and I have to mine. Now do you begin to understand the joy that makes God glad?

One evening, years ago, I found myself returning unexpectedly to my summer cottage on Cape Cod after having been several weeks away from it. I was eager to reach my family, and I grew ever more impatient with the talkative bus driver as we drove away from our railroad station. He was a man new to me. Then he broke into his real story and I was at once interested. "Some excitement on the beach this morning," he said. "Two boys blown out to sea on a raft that broke up." "Who were the boys?" I asked. And the driver replied, "Well, one of them was Poling's kid."

I shall never live long enough to forget the horror that swept me, the agony that I lived through until I learned that one of my brothers had reached and rescued those two small fellows just before their frail raft, upon which they had stolen away to play, broke up.

When the child is yours, you suffer—and you rejoice when he is saved. Now I know why the single returned prodigal makes God glad. For he—and every prodigal son and daughter —is God's child.

27. THE QUEST FOR WISDOM

JESUS SAYS: *Get thee behind me, Satan....*
LUKE 4:8

It has been said that the first part of wisdom is to discern that which is false, the second to know that which is true. Jesus in His ministry was forever separating the false from the true. How often he had to point out the wrong, uncover the sophistry, and say "Get thee behind me, Satan." In His wilderness temptations—and there were three of these: hunger of the body, hunger of the mind, and hunger of the soul—Jesus made for Himself the ultimate decision and gave to His followers the guideposts for theirs.

How sensitive Jesus was to the false note wherever it was sounded! To his disciples on Palm Sunday, the waving branches and cheers were confirmation of the final triumph. Already they saw themselves by the side of their Master in seats of the mighty. But the silent Rider on the humble beast was not deceived. Again He recognized the false notes, but He rode on.

Jesus knew men, but also He knew Himself. He knew the source of His power and He knew, too, that those who followed Him could draw upon that power if they would search it out, wait for it, and receive it. Life's greatest adventure, the greatest of all quests, is the quest for wisdom, which is the high goal of knowledge. "Happy is the man that findeth wisdom, and the man that getteth understanding," the book of Proverbs tells us. And the wisdom referred to is the knowledge of God, His will and His way, which carries in its heart always true happiness and security.

A forest fire may sweep the timber from the ranges and leave a man, once rated a millionaire, penniless. A ship may founder at sea and carry down to the shells of the ocean bed its owner's wealth. Your stocks rise and fall with the fluctuating prices of an uncertain market. But wisdom needs no lock to hold it safe from any thief. Floods do not drown it, fires never consume it, and temporary adversity cannot carry it away. It is permanent. Being of the mind, it is the only treasure that accompanies you beyond the grave. It is the capital with which we begin business in the next world.

Our absolute and detailed knowledge of God may be limited. Indeed, when we accept the "Divinity that rules us all," we also accept the limitations of our finite minds, and in this acceptance we find the crown of faith. But while our detailed knowledge of God may be limited, this we do know: God is good as well as great, God is love, and God is able. His attitude toward us, as Jesus Christ has revealed Him to us, is that of a limitless Father desiring our best. He moves with love through every experience that may come to us to complete our lives and to perfect our happiness. This we know about God, or this we may know. This knowledge we have, or may have. This is wisdom, and it is enough.

I had a friend who lost his fortune and his business in the crash of 1929. When I visited him in 1931 I was prepared for a change in him that I did not find. He was now living above the garage on his old estate. But he greeted me with nearly all of his old buoyant manner. We talked of many things—about the past, and the present, but chiefly of his plans for the immediate future. These were definite and well within practical realization. I saw that his faith—faith in God, in his country, in himself, and particularly in his wife, who was standing stanchly by his side—had strengthened in adversity.

As we walked to the station, we passed through the town square. My friend stopped me, pointed beyond the intervening buildings to the hospital he had given his town, and said, "Dan, I still have that—and all the rest!" And in this spirit, with the basic wisdom he had not lost, this man went steadily forward to new and even greater success than he had known before.

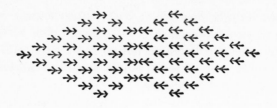

28. THE GLORY OF
GRATITUDE

JESUS SAYS: ...*where are the nine?*
LUKE 17:17

The healing of ten lepers, as the story is told in Luke, is one of the most vivid and meaningful of all the miracles of Jesus recorded in the New Testament. The fact that only one of the ten men, and that one a despised Samaritan, turned back to thank Jesus is as vivid as the miracle itself. Ten men had faith and cried, "Jesus, Master, have mercy on us." Their faith made instant response when the Master answered, "Go shew yourselves unto the priests." They fairly leaped to action. But only one, a stranger in that company of the chosen, the Samaritan, had a gratitude so profound that he expressed it.

There were extenuating circumstances, of course. Imagine yourself for months and perhaps years buried alive, shut away from your loved ones. Imagine yourself a rotting ruin of a man and then imagine yourself healed in the twinkling of an eye and given your key to "Home, Sweet Home." I can see those nine men with the first rush of healthy blood to their limbs look incredulously upon their new fingers, lift their hands to faces restored, and in the half-hypnotism of a child's Christmas ecstasy, with a cry of utter joy, rush off to show themselves to their nearest and their dearest.

Yes, of a kind, there are excuses aplenty for the nine, only there is no excuse after all. There is never an excuse for ingratitude. Certainly they could not have found words with which to express their hearts, but they could have tried. All that one did the others might have done. But it is frequently the case that gratitude is found in strangers rather than among the chosen. And too many of us forget to give thanks for one blessing before we ask for another, like the small boy to whom an apple was given by a kind lady. His mother urged him to say "thank you." To her chagrin, the lad fairly shouted, "Have you got any more?"

The glory of gratitude is threefold: glory for the receiver, glory for the giver, and glory for the observer. The grateful leper made the soul of Jesus glad as he flung himself at the Master's blistered feet. His own soul was near bursting with his praise and those who saw his act had mists upon their eyes that were like fleecy clouds the rising sun has kissed with gold. Nor let it be forgotten that the outcast Samaritan received an even greater gift than physical healing when he turned back. He heard the words the nine would never hear: "Arise, go thy way: thy faith hath made thee whole." It is the supreme glory of gratitude that it increases the very blessings that call it forth.

Gratitude is a spirit, a livening spirit, a spirit that becomes vocal, that multiplies like the rising notes of a deep-toned bell. Gratitude is greater than faith. Faith brought healing to ten lepers, but gratitude brought one of them to Jesus. Faith healed the body; gratitude perfected the soul. Gratitude is, in essence, love. "And now abideth faith, hope, love, and the greatest of these is love." Would you be one of the few? Of course! But best be the Samaritan who turned back to Jesus with gratitude in his heart.

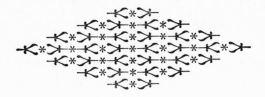

29. THE CONQUEST OF FEAR

JESUS SAYS: *Fear not....*
LUKE 12:32

Jesus constantly assured and reassured His friends and followers. They were often afraid—and with good reason. The authorities of their Church were against them and the Roman masters of their little land were against them. They had no "economic security." The One they loved and followed could give them nothing tangible; indeed He promised them only hardships, dangers, and the assurance that at last He Himself would leave them. In the chapter of St. Luke from which the words "fear not" are taken, Jesus again and again speaks out against fear. "Be not afraid of them that kill the body ..." He tells His followers. He assures them that their physical well-being is secondary, that the soul is immortal, and that evil men cannot destroy it. Then he concludes, "Fear not, little flock, for it is your Father's good pleasure to give you the kingdom." In other words, you cannot fail if you are true.

And today, here and now, this is the assurance of Jesus Christ to those who hear His voice and follow Him.

The greatest of all victories is the conquest of fear. Once I found one of my small children in front of our summer cottage, jumping up and down in a veritable frenzy of fear and shouting at the top of her lungs, "I'm not afraid! I'm not afraid! I'm not afraid!" At her feet sat a tiny brown tree toad.

Doubtless a good many of us, to ourselves at least, have shouted like that. A thousand fears surround us. Walking through New York City's vast canyons of streets, an old gentleman from the West was heard to say, "I certainly would not want to live around here, for she is bound to fall, she is bound to fall." You and I need to hear the voice Peter and James and John and the rest heard: "Fear not...."

I was once asked whether I thought courage could be cultivated or acquired, whether I did not think we were born with it if we had it or were to possess it. I replied that I do not believe fearless men and women are always born fearless. I am inclined to think that Peter, who heard Jesus say "Fear not," was a born coward and that his natural gait was flight. He developed a good deal of his speed in getting away from difficult situations. Peter found his courage when he found his Master.

If in the quiet of your innermost soul you know that you are a coward, remember Peter. Study the thing through, God helping you (and He will); reach a conclusion; and then stand straight and tall for a principle or a cause. When Jesus said, "Fear not...for it is your Father's good pleasure to give you...," He meant that He would give courage, courage that comes with faith in Him, courage of the highest and most permanent quality, courage that can encounter successfully the loss of friends, the loss even of a good name if one is falsely accused, courage that can face, as Peter faced it, a world full of scorn and hate, courage that can see the prosperity of years swept away—courage that can see and know all of this and fight on, fearless still.

Not long ago, a friend of mine who was used to administering large affairs with great success suddenly faced financial ruin. The details do not belong here, but at least some of his trouble was concerned with the tens of thousands of dollars he had invested in bringing European refugees to this country. When the crisis was passed and we again met and prayed together, he said, "I asked God to keep me from fear and He did." Fear would have destroyed this man. He did every last thing within his power to meet his problems, and then he put his trust in the higher power, saying, "I will trust and not be afraid."

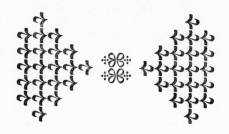

30. THE LIGHT
THAT NEVER FAILS

JESUS SAYS: *I am the light of the world....*

JOHN 8:12

Jesus had just completed His remarkable interview with the adulterous woman who was brought to Him by a crowd of eager Pharisees who proposed that she be stoned to death. He had just finished saying "...go, and sin no more" when He declared, "I am the light of the world: he that followeth me shall not walk in darkness, but shall have the light of life." Some men seem to find a contradiction between this emphatic "I am the light of the world" and His equally emphatic declaration, "Ye are the light of the world." But certainly there is no contradiction. We can be the light of the world only because He is the light of the world and because He, being in us, shines out through us. How perfectly this marvelous relationship between the human and the divine was portrayed when, at the healing of a blind man, Jesus said, "As long as I am in

86

the world, I am the light of the world." Almost I hear Him continue, "and when I am no longer physically in the world, I must rely upon you. Then you must be the light of the world."

To be a Christian is a terrible responsibility. A failing beacon on Cape Cod means a ship on the shoals, and a Christian gone astray may lead another life to shipwreck. Do you then refuse to accept the invitation to become a Christian? Or do you hesitate? But you really escape nothing. The responsibility as well as the opportunity remains, but by your own choice you may keep your beacon unlighted and unburning. The only complete failure is the failure of one who refuses to try.

I do not know what darkness of doubt or uncertainty, of grief or disappointment, may surround you, but I do know that Jesus is the light and that He can make plain a way ahead for you. Friends advise and cheer us, friends comfort and strengthen us, but the best advice ever given me by a friend I received many years ago, when I was in college. It was to put my trust, my life, my all in the keeping of the One Who said, "I am the light of the world: he that followeth me shall not walk in darkness, but shall have the light of life."

Down in Wall Street, in the front of the old Sub-Treasury Building, is a bas-relief of a man kneeling in prayer. His time was one of fear and great darkness. The cause to which he had dedicated his life, for which he had led brave men to death, seemed sinking fast into a night of irretrievable disaster. Burdens seemingly too heavy to be borne rested upon him. But he did not retreat; he did not resign. For a moment he turned aside. It was very dark. The way had eluded him. And so he stopped, knelt in the snows at Valley Forge, and looked up. And then George Washington set his course again by the great light. When he rose from his knees he had the answer, and with that answer and following in that light, under God, he gave freedom a new name and liberty a new destiny.

And it is precisely this approach, direct and immediate, as we kneel in the snows of our own Valley Forges, that will bring to us the spiritual reinforcements that will provide the courage and strength and power for our own ordeals.

31. WHEN EVIL HASTENS GOOD

JESUS SAYS: *Father, forgive them; for they know not what they do.*
LUKE 23:34

"Evil wastes itself," it has been said. In childhood violent tempers are quickly spent, and in adult society the more vicious elements do not long endure, since they arouse opposition very quickly. Chapman wrote, in *The History of Man,* "It has been very generally the case that when evils have grown insufferable they have touched the point of cure." A wild mob out of legal control destroyed the physical life of Jesus, but His ministry was given better than a double speed forward by His death. And in the spirit of His cry, "Father, forgive them," was the redemption of man. They thought they "knew" but they knew not what they did that day.

Unchecked wrath and violent will rushing forward under a free rein generally defeat their own purpose. Joseph's brothers had no idea of creating a prime minister when they sold him to merchants bound for Egypt, but their jealousy made a prince

instead of a prisoner. Then in a later dynasty, Pharaoh's crafty avarice in putting yet heavier burdens upon the Hebrews caused him to lose them, although for a time he may have obtained more bricks. In the end, slaves who under a more generous servitude might have remained with the fleshpots forever went on famine rations to discover a promised land beyond the wilderness.

Always evil hastens good. Though dueling in America lasted well through the nineteenth century, we can say that the practice received a mortal blow when Burr slew Hamilton. There is a homely saying which runs "Give a calf enough rope and it will choke itself." The principle applies far beyond the barnyard. The crucifixion of Jesus was not a triumph for the crucifiers.

Does all of this not indicate that humankind is not the mere sport of chance, that we are not at the mercy of the ruthless, whether these be passions within or foes without?

"The wrath of men shall praise Him" is a sublime text. Somewhere I have read that the musician's harp came from the warrior's bow. We do not always live to see a great principle vindicated, for man is a creature of generations, while truth endures for eternity. History teaches us that in its most unbridled excesses man's wrath and hate work toward the ultimate purposes of the Infinite Good Will.

Of this the supreme example is the crucifixion. Man's wrath led Jesus to a Roman judgment, planned His execution, nailed together His cross, swung Him high between earth and heaven, tortured Him to a physical death, and sealed Him in a tomb—but "by His stripes we are healed!" From that dark day on Calvary until now man's most terrible doings have had their share in setting in motion God's most gracious ministries.

Thus evil hastens good. Thus defeat may point the way to victory. Thus hardship may strengthen us to master mountains, and in ways that beggar description men and women achieve the faith that overcomes the world. "God moves in a mysterious way His wonders to perform."

As a very small instance of how good may come from evil, or how a bitter disappointment may turn into an advantage, I shall always remember an incident of my boyhood. Wishing to go to sea, I found a job on a freighter bound for Tokyo. Immediately I was the envy of all my young friends in Portland, Oregon. Then came the war between Russia and Japan. My parents refused to let me sail. I rebelled and went to see the captain, but he would not—could not—take me without my father's consent. Later, we heard that the freighter struck a mine in the Sea of Japan and went down with all hands.

32. WHAT WE NEED MOST

JESUS SAYS: *The hour is come, that the Son of man should be glorified.*

JOHN 12:23

These and the poignant words following them, some of the most profoundly moving words spoken by Jesus, were in answer to the famous request of the Greeks addressed to Philip: "Sir, we would see Jesus." What a strange answer! And stranger still these following words: "He that loveth his life shall lose it; and he that hateth his life in this world shall keep it unto life eternal." And, continuing, "If any man serve me, let him follow me;...him will my Father honour." The climax was reached when Jesus cried, "Father, glorify thy name." And then came a voice from Heaven, saying, "I have both glorified it, and will glorify it again." All of this happened shortly before the events associated with the Passover feast in Jerusalem, which immediately preceded Christ's betrayal, trial, conviction, and execution.

But this important request of the Greeks is the heart of the matter that concerns us today. The first immediate desire, if not the supreme need of these Greeks, was to "see" Jesus. And this need is our supreme need today. We have many needs—food and water, oxygen and sleep—just for physical survival. And we need recreation, friends, and work to know the more abundant life. But give us nothing more than these and we shall not exceed a mere existence, we shall not achieve a truly abundant life. All of the physical and even intellectual and social necessities are not in themselves enough. For man has come from God and his soul is restless until it rests in Him. And so after he has known every other gift to body and mind, man comes at last as came the Greeks to Philip, with the importunate request "Sir, we would see Jesus." See Him, too, in spite of the grave words He spoke concerning His own "glory road" of suffering, which He made clear was the road to be traveled by those who came to see Him and remained to follow with Him.

We would see *Jesus*—not the disciples, but Jesus. We would see Jesus, for He alone can cover our sins and frustrations with the divine alchemy of His forgiveness and forgetfulness. We would see Jesus, for He alone can give us peace of mind. We would see Jesus, for He alone can satisfy our insatiate thirst. We would see Jesus of the Samaritan well who promises "Whosoever shall drink of this water shall thirst again; but whosoever drinketh of the water I shall give him shall never thirst; but the water that I shall give him shall be in him a well of water springing up into everlasting life."

One further point—and it is essential. The Greeks who came to see Jesus sought an introduction from one who knew Him. In my college years a remarkable man came quietly into my life. He did his best to teach me the German language and the skills of public speaking. Perhaps he did not completely fail, but chiefly I revere his memory because he lived before me and others a life that was absolutely a model. One evening as this good and truly great man came smiling toward us under the oak trees, the friend with whom I was standing said, "There comes Jesus Christ on the feet of David Metzger."

The supreme business of the Christian Church at all times is introducing men and women and society to Jesus Christ—and only those who know Him themselves are competent to introduce others to Him. "Sir, we would see Jesus," is the cry of a rocking world today, the importunate call of troubled men and women of all races and conditions—and they are talking not to Philip but to me and to you.

33. EXTREMITY AND OPPORTUNITY

JESUS SAYS: *...the hour is at hand....*
MATTHEW 26:45

Jesus spoke these words in the garden of Gethsemane just before His betrayal. Now He was the central figure in the supreme paradox of time. He was helpless and He was all-sufficient. He was defeated and He was triumphant. He was on the road of humiliation, facing Calvary, and His feet had begun to press the glory path that led to His coronation. He was at the extremity of His humanity and about to accept the opportunity of deity. As a teacher He was rejected; as Pilate's king of the Jews He was denied; but as Savior of the world He was mounting to His spiritual throne.

Today man is close to the hour of his extremity. He has made machines that can destroy him and his world, but he has not mastered himself. He stands on top of his world, ready to conquer outer space, but he holds a bomb in his hand and he is afraid as he has never been afraid before. He does not fear the bomb; he fears himself—fears that he will drop the bomb.

But man's extremity is God's opportunity. And however I may describe and declare Him, whatever my definition of God may be, surely my conclusion is the conclusion of the young Scotsman in World War I who wrote his mother only a few days before he died while gallantly leading his men in a charge, "God must be." In one vivid paragraph he spoke of the inadequacy of everything his eyes had seen or his mind could conjure, and concluded with the words "Mother, God must be." And today are we not face to face with extremity's conclusion, which is also extremity's compulsion? "God must be." It was in the hour at hand, the hour of Christ's extremity, that God came to Him, and so He comes to us. No other mind but His can shape the answer to our questions. No other love than His can heal our wounds, allay our suspicions, quench our spiritual thirsts, comfort our sorrows, conquer our hates, forgive our sins, and at last raise our dead. God *must* be.

But for such a time as this, how and where shall we find God? Easter has the answer. We find God at Calvary and in the Resurrection; we find God in Jesus Christ, His Son, who is—or, if we choose to claim Him, will become—our Lord and Savior.

Who is Jesus? He has the answer for that question. "I am the way, the truth, and the life." And with the answer He extends the gracious invitation "Come unto me, all ye that labour and are heavy laden, and I will give you rest."

This is the invitation, all-inclusive, universal. But it has an alternative. Above the scarred and suffering world, the world shaken by its fears today, He flings His words against our flaming skies: "Without me ye can do nothing." He alone can equalize social inequities, destroy racial hates, bring the world back from its competitive armament madness to that regard of each for the other without which no freedom is secure. And how will He do this? By changing man himself. By making the new world with new men and new women. This is the Easter message and the Easter faith and these are its words of reassurance and triumph: "Fear not, I am with thee."

For seventeen years I was closely associated with George Bolton, the superintendent of the Bowery Mission in New York City. When George came to America from England he was a wandering derelict and gambler. Soon he reached his hour of physical and moral extremity. Feeling himself a doomed man without hope of recovery, he nevertheless entered a mission on the Bowery and knelt and prayed. And seeking God, he found Him. When George Bolton rose from that altar the miracle of redemption had happened, and he was a new man. Back to him came his heartbroken, faithful wife. With her and their children he lived that miracle on one of the saddest streets of the world, giving of himself to lead thousands of other derelicts into the new life as new men.

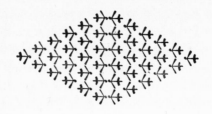

34. WHAT GOD
DOES NOT PROMISE

JESUS SAYS: *I will not leave you comfortless:*
I will come to you.
JOHN 14:18

This promise comes from the "upper room" in Jerusalem where Jesus had the Last Supper with His disciples and where He spoke the most intimate of all words that ever fell from His inspired lips.

God never promises exemption. He does promise companionship, which is better. He does not promise to deliver you or me or any other individual from pain, sorrow, economic disaster, or any other misfortune. But He does give the assurance that He will help us through and that there will be compensations. "I will not leave you comfortless," Jesus promised; "I will come to you." That promise is eternal.

And this more needs saying: Nowhere in either the Old Testament or the New are we assured special well-being because of our piety. Indeed, there are instances, as in the great drama of Job, when goodness itself is tested and made a vehicle of trial. Even Paul cried to be relieved of his "thorn in the flesh," but cried in vain; and his contemporaries, the disciples, including Peter and the faithful who were hunted through the Roman catacombs and burned along the Appian Way and fed to the lions in the Colosseum, were not relieved of their physical ordeals because they were holy. But that never-disregarded promise, "I will come to you," was kept with each of them and it is written that they chose to suffer affliction rather than to enjoy what Rome at her voluptuous best had to offer. In Paul's Epistle to the Hebrews it is even more baldly stated: "For whom the Lord loveth he chasteneth, and scourgeth every son whom he receiveth." Surely these are words hard to understand. Indeed, they are not to be understood this side of that "time enough" of which the great Horace Bushnell of Yale spoke— that unhurried eternal moment when the hidden things shall be revealed and when we shall find the answers for the questions remaining unanswered and for the problems yet unsolved.

The appalling suffering of the best, the eminent, and the good—the problem of human suffering itself—remains as the great unsolvable of time, nor do I ever blink that issue. But this I do know. God comes to these and grants them mercies and foregleams of that which is theirs presently to possess. I have seen them in veritable ecstasies upon their deathbeds. We might reasonably curse and die as Job's friends recommended to him, if this life were all. Those who believe it to be all and who so insist are to be understood when they curse. But this life is definitely not all! This knowledge, this faith, is for the one who writes these sentences an experience. It may be yours. I have known again and again, in peace as in war, beside my dying loved ones and during an illness of my own that was all but final, the fulfillment of the promise: "I will not leave you comfortless: I will come to you."

How may you know the same promise? "Ask and ye shall receive." It is as simple and yet as profound as that. A whispered prayer, a prayer not even whispered but in the mind, will bring to you this comfort, this reassurance.

As these lines are written I have just come from a visit with the friend of my boyhood and lifetime, Dr. Chester Paul Gates. We were in college together; we began our pledged ministry together. Chester went on to become an eloquent and dynamic preacher and church administrator. Now the victim of chronic illness, all but helpless he waits expectantly on that last clear call that will crown his life's work. As the time came for me to depart from his quiet room, I said, "Chester, this time you pray." And then, with my head bowed above his chair, I listened to him pray as he had never prayed in his days of strength. It was a prayer of triumph. Not a prayer for deliverance from weakness and pain, it was a prayer of gratitude for the presence of the Great Companion, a prayer in which the glory of Chester's own assured faith filled the room and possessed my soul. Chester Gates was not left comfortless.

35. PALMS OR VICTORY

JESUS SAYS: *My house shall be called the house of prayer; but ye have made it a den of thieves.*

MATTHEW 21:13

It was immediately following the triumphal entry of Jesus into Jerusalem that He went into the Temple and "cast out all them that sold and bought in the temple, and overthrew the tables of the moneychangers, and the seats of them that sold doves." Then Jesus said, "... My house shall be called the house of prayer; but ye have made it a den of thieves."

This was the morning when "the multitudes that went before, and that followed, cried, saying, Hosanna to the Son of David: Blessed is He that cometh in the name of the Lord: Hosanna in the highest." And some of the people spread their garments in the way, while others cut down branches from the trees and laid them before the little beast upon which He rode. Perhaps He could have captured the city that day, and re-established the kingdom of His fathers. But for Him the choice had long since been made. He did not—could not—accept the palms; He was bound to claim the spiritual victory that rejected the plaudits of the people. And how quickly He began His rule! Immediately He went about the unpopular business of "cleansing" the holy place, the house of worship that avaricious men had defiled. In one short sentence He stated the case and gave the reason for His act of violence.

This day we know as Palm Sunday was the day of test, the great test for Jesus. Now upon His shoulders rested the heavy load of abnegation and into His soul entered the iron of self-denial. Not palms and victory for Him—for Him the alternative was palms *or* victory. Had He listened to the wildly cheering multitude that day, He might have overthrown the puppet of Caesar, He might have given Israel another Golden Age and left a name to stand with that of David and Solomon. But after that? Had He yielded, they would have had at the most another conquering monarch instead of the world's Savior and Redeemer.

At the close of a Lenten service in Philadelphia more than a generation ago, a man who was to me as one risen from the dead grasped my hand. As a resident physician and surgeon in Detroit but under appointment as a medical missionary to China, he had once found himself facing this same alternative: palms or victory. He had begun laboratory research work that had opened to him the facilities of great American institutions. The future of a life in the United States made him great promises. Instead, he went to China.

Bits of news came back to his family and friends. His scalpel was a magic wand. The blind saw, the deaf heard, the lame walked. The struggles of the warlords in Hunan, the raids of bandits seemed to have no terrors for him. His wards were full and to him, whatever the flags they followed, all who suffered were as brothers. Then came the great offensive, when forces in the south moved north. Reluctantly the young surgeon left his operating room to plant himself in the entrance of the hospital he had opened as a door of hope to a hopeless people. Literally, his body blocked that door. When the war front moved on, the body of my friend bore wounds as heroic as ever opened the veins of man.

Now, as I met him in Philadelphia, he was in the United States for an operation and medical care he could not get in China. Only this, and then he would return. When I gripped his hand that day, it was the hand of another who had taken the way of victory instead of palms.

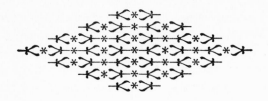

36. MOTHERHOOD'S CONSTANCY

Jesus SAYS: *Woman, behold thy son!*

JOHN 19:26

About the story of the first of the recorded miracles of Jesus many controversies have raged. But for me the marriage at Cana in Galilee, where the miracle was performed, has its chief interest in the fact that Mary, the mother of Jesus, was there.

We know little enough of this blessed woman. Eagerly we search the Scriptures for every bit of information concerning her. But there is something very reassuring about the fact that she was present at this marriage feast. We know now that her life was not altogether heavy and colorless, that she was a woman of moods, that she must have smiled. Picture the young life of Cana gathered to wish the bride and groom a happy future; remember that Jesus Himself came to the celebration; and then gather a truer perspective for your final judgment as to the life and character of Mary as you read, "the mother of Jesus was there."

We know, of course, that often in the flesh, as always in her spirit, Mary was with her Son in the great ordeals and moments of His life. There is nothing written to *prove* that she saw Him ride in triumph down lanes of wildly cheering men, women, and children on Palm Sunday, but I have no doubt that she saw Him then. "The mother of Jesus was there!" She saw it all. And what mixed emotions must have possessed her as the sunlight streamed across the face and form of One whose baby lips had drawn life from her breasts. Do not strong men testify that chiefly their mothers are responsible for their greatness? Garfield, immediately after his lips had rested upon the Bible and he had taken his oath as President of the United States, turned, stooped, and kissed the gray-haired woman who had borne him. Lincoln affirmed "All that I am, all that I ever hope to be, I owe to my angel mother." Yes, on Palm Sunday, Mary was there. I am sure of that.

And now three crosses stand in blood, heavily weighted with their crop of death against the darkened sky on Calvary. It is the Crucifixion. Through Gethsemane and the howling mob in Pilate's trial chamber and through bitter insults in the courtroom of Ananias, through the denials of Peter, the jeers of the fickle populace, Jesus has come to His ignominious death. Words can hardly picture the catastrophe, but "the mother of Jesus was there." Close to the cross; near enough to hear the words that fell from the lips of her dying Son; near enough to see the play of agony upon His face; near enough to clasp His suffering feet and feel upon her hands the hot blood from His wounds. So near that she heard, as John the beloved disciple heard, "Woman, behold thy son!"—and heard too the instruction given John: "Behold thy mother!"

Mary was there, at the foot of the cross on that "green hill outside the city gate." And for me the knowledge that she saw her Son in the final moments of His agony and did not turn away is one of the most poignant aspects of the Good Friday drama. And it is much more. It is the symbol of the sublime quality of motherhood through the ages. At the foot of every cross upon which their sons and daughters have suffered, we have seen their mothers. And evermore the mothers will be there.

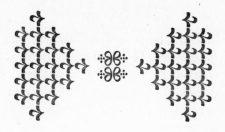

37. THE WOUNDS
OF A FRIEND

JESUS SAYS: *The cock shall not crow, till thou hast denied me thrice.*

JOHN 13:38

With these hard words Jesus greeted the heroic avowal of Peter, "I will lay down my life for thy sake." And within a few hours Peter had done just that as he stood in the courtyard of the High Priest's palace: denied his Friend, His Lord and Master Who was a prisoner, now bound and condemned by His enemies. It is recorded that conscience-stricken Peter "wept bitterly." Up from that sad defeat Peter rose to win his way back into the confidence of Jesus and to merit the vast spiritual honors that have come to him because of his ever-faithful loyalty, loyalty to the death. Wounded by his Friend Who accurately foretold his human weaknesses, Peter became a man of incomparable courage and achievement.

But true friends do not nag—do not say their say over and over again. Confucius wisely observed that "between friends frequent reproach makes the friendship distant." How detestable is the fellow, brazen and self-satisfied, who goes about saying, "You know me; I'm plainspoken, frank, candid." Pity the people who feel themselves anointed to pass out wounds, small and large indiscriminately, who seem to regard generous speaking and praise as associated with original sin!

But the Apostle Paul was fine and brave, utterly courageous, when he said to his friends and intimates in the churches who had turned away from his teachings and denied his leadership, "Am I therefore become your enemy because I tell you the truth?" Speaking the truth, Paul was now disliked because he inflicted pain, but the pain was a clear symptom of a more serious trouble, trouble that would not be cured by cursing Paul. Like a skilled physician, the apostle had placed his finger upon the sore spot and the patient had cowered away from the touch with an angry glance at the doctor. Pity the patient when he falls into the hands of a surgeon who is less than honest. Perhaps the keenest suffering we ever know comes to us when in love we inflict pain upon one loved, when we hurt to heal.

A little girl—our daughter Rachel—who had escaped the more serious results of an automobile accident was found to have developed infections in what had at first appeared to be superficial scratches and bruises. The physician insisted that twice daily the wounds must be vigorously washed, scrubbed with a disinfectant; for scabs to be allowed to form before the infection had been completely conquered and the wounds had healed soundly from beneath would mean scars and permanent disfigurement. The ordeal for the child was a sternly painful one. Though half-frantic at times, she was very brave and determined. There were moments when she fairly tore at the hands inflicting beneficient torture upon her, but never did she misunderstand the purpose behind them nor cry out against the nurse and doctor. Today her lovely face is without a single blemish. The hurts that healed the child were from the hands of her friends and loved ones. The hurt in the words of Jesus when He rebuked Peter made Peter a conquering hero of the Christian faith.

38. THE GREATEST FACT
OF HISTORY

JESUS SAYS: *And I, if I be lifted up from the earth,
will draw all men unto me.*

JOHN 12:32

The greatness of Christianity is found in the uniqueness of its
method. Perhaps the most amazing words ever spoken by a
leader were these: "...if I be lifted up from the earth, I will
draw all men unto me." For, as it is written in the Scriptures,
"This he said, signifying what death he should die." Jesus was
describing the cross and the ignominious death of His crucifixion. And He would win with this! With what seemed a
defeat, a final human disaster. As it proved, he won with
sacrifice and love.

All other conquerors came upon the scene with power and
force. Lashes in the hands of brutal slavedrivers herded the
minions of Xerxes, a million strong, into the pass at Ther-
mopylae; terror ran before the hordes of Genghis Khan and
Attila; fear and power in a thousand hidden forms have been

the bulwark of every jungle worship. But Jesus, Who today stands supreme in the hungry hearts of a billion human souls, when He laid before His lieutenants His final campaign and gave them directions that were to continue through time and space, said, "...if I be lifted up from the earth, I will draw all men unto me." "Not by might, nor by power, but by my spirit, saith the Lord of hosts." And in the last analysis Christianity is great and powerful because it is a spirit. And because it captures, commands, controls the spirits of men.

What confirmation that promise of Jesus that He would draw all men has had! They swung Him up between earth and sky, between thieves, on a criminal's cross. But with the last breath of His "It is finished" began the disintegration of the Roman Empire. They stoned Stephen, and one of that very company of murderous persecutors, Saul of Tarsus, became Paul, the field marshal of His advance toward the earth's last frontiers. They fed His faithful followers to lions they had starved to make a spectacle for the Roman populace. And presently the reddened sand of the Colosseum became the seed-ground of His Church, for "the blood of martyrs is the seed of the Church." And as persecutions continued they burned His book, only to discover that they had unchained His word.

At last, when persecution and martyrdom had failed, popularity came to more seriously threaten His plan. Constantine saw the cross in the sky, and multitudes took upon themselves His name in easy fashion, hiding their true selves behind their loud professions. Wealth and position turned the heads of His captains: the Church herself became corrupt in her human leadership.

But though shaken to its foundations, His cause did not fall, and today, with perilous times behind and perilous times ahead,

His spirit raises an irresistible tide in human affairs, bearing man forward, drawing him upward and on.

In all history there is not another spectacle like this: a king without a capital, with a crown of thorns and a cross for a throne, a conqueror without an army, an empire without a sword. The fact is proof that love at last is indeed the greatest thing in the world. Christ's formula for conquest is unique and He is the greatest fact of history.

And this same Conqueror Who was first proclaimed "King of Kings and Lord of Lords" and then crucified between two criminals, all within a week, is your Savior and mine, here and now. He is at once universal and personal, and in His personal ministry to me He is not the crucified Prophet of Nazareth but the risen, living Lord of life—my life. So may He be to you.

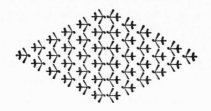

39. DEAD KING OR LIVING LORD?

J ESUS SAYS: *Why are ye troubled?*
LUKE 24:38

These words, spoken by Jesus to His eleven disciples who waited in fear and discouraged grief after His crucifixion and entombment, were the beginning of the great reassurance that He brought to them with His risen presence.

The supreme question of Easter morning is not "Did Jesus rise?" but "Is Jesus risen?" Eternal hope, the hope of our Christian faith, trembles in the balance as we turn our eyes toward the tomb in Joseph's garden where Mary hurried through the dews of that first Easter dawn, and as we hear the message she heard—the stupendous question, "Why seek ye the living among the dead?"

What does Easter mean to us? Why are we troubled, if we are? As we look back upon that event and lose the sense of time and space, what does the heavenly spokesman who spoke to Mary say to us? What is the message here and now? "He

rose" or "He is risen"? He was or He is? The tense is everything. Our peace of mind, our moral health, our bravest hope
for life, life eternal, depend upon our answer to that question.

The ultimate challenge, then, is "Dead king or living Lord?"

He was not a dead king Who lighted signal fires in the
Pentecostal upper room, Who commanded the intrepid sons
and daughters of the early Church. He was not a dead king
Who took command of Saul of Tarsus, Who at last conquered Rome more completely than did the barbarians—and
Who has today set up a spiritual empire more potent than that
of any conqueror from Alexander the Great, the Caesars, or
Attila to Napoleon and Lenin and Hitler. He was not a dead
king Who went before the Cross of Augustine and tamed the
fires for Savonarola and Huss and so many others—tamed
them even when they consumed. He was not a dead king Who
guided the Pilgrims on the *Mayflower* and the Dutch on the
Half Moon across practically uncharted seas to North America
and Who then opened the wilderness and evangelized the con-
tinent from the Atlantic to the Pacific. Pilate was wrong; the
priests of Jerusalem were wrong; the curious onlookers, the
disappointed spectators were wrong; the disciples and Mary
were wrong. All were mistaken. He was not dead when on
the cross His body died. He was then as He is now, and
evermore shall be, the living Lord.

For me, this is the message of Easter, and while it underlies
the entire structure of Christian faith, and while it is the most
profound theological element of our religion, it has a warmth
in its personal application, an intimate tenderness, that makes
it healing for a harassed mind and wounded spirit, and a song
in the night to a sorrowing soul.

When I beheld my mother for the last time before we turned

back the sod and tucked her body under, she whispered to me: "My son, if when you come again and do not find me waiting, as always before I have been waiting for you, then you will know where to find me." And I do know where I shall find her.

Jesus Christ is the living Lord. In spite of time and change, still with the ardor of my youth, of those years when faith first came to build an altar in my heart, I answer all my doubts and fears, heal all my hurts, with "He is risen." And I am not afraid.

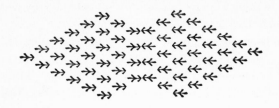

40. WAITING FOR POWER

JESUS SAYS: *...tarry ye in the city of Jerusalem, until ye be endued with power....*

LUKE 24:49

These words of Jesus were spoken to His disciples on the occasion of His last meeting with them. He ate with them and urged them to look closely in order that they should be convinced that He was not a "ghost." "Handle me, and see," He told them: "for a spirit hath not flesh and bones, as ye see me have." Jesus went on then to "open their understanding," that they might understand the Scriptures. Then, Luke tells us, "...he led them out as far as to Bethany, and he lifted up his hands, and blessed them. And it came to pass ...he was parted from them, and carried up into heaven." That was a triumphant hour for the disciples: "...they worshipped him, and returned to Jerusalem with great joy." And following the instructions they had received in that last physical meeting with their Lord, obedient to His command, they tarried in Jerusalem, waiting in prayer and fellowship until, as they had been promised, they were "endued with power...."

The power that came to these humble and unlettered men was of such quality and degree that it made them each a veritable Hercules of courage and achievement. After their waiting time had passed, they were equipped and ready to face a world of unbelief, to risk and undergo humiliation, imprisonment, torture, and death for their faith. They were ready to rise from their knees and stride out across all physical frontiers as witnesses for Him Whose love they had experienced, and Whose cause they had espoused. They would now make Him and His cause known to men and women of all races and conditions to the ends of the earth.

A poet has written:

> The hardest thing is just to wait—
> This is the agonizing fate.

And often the hardest thing in our praying is waiting for the answer. Of course this may be because we already have the answer—our answer. We pray not to have God's answer but to have Him confirm the answer we have already prepared for ourselves. Prayer is or should be a two-way conversation. And of course in such a conversation with God, listening— waiting—is more important than talking. Prayer is communion and it was in communion with God that the disciples tarried after returning from Bethany and their last joyous physical experience with Jesus. Power was the answer then! And power is the answer now for those who wait, those who tarry and listen.

Traveling by train from Louisville to Cincinnati many years ago, I sat with closed eyes and my face pressed against the window. I was troubled, frustrated, uncertain. I was facing up to a major decision in my life and I could find no words with which to express my prayer, though prayer seemed now my only alternative to a major defeat. And so, almost in desperation, I waited. I was silent with a deep inner silence. I was completely relaxed, utterly unconscious of my surroundings. Though another traveler sat by my side, I was alone, as much alone as though I were a thousand miles removed from those close about me. Then came the answer! Then came reassurance. That answer possessed me—body, mind, and spirit. I left the train in Cincinnati a new man and went out to meet successfully the ordeal I had dreaded and for which I had, until I waited, absolutely nothing to offer.

Wait—listen. The method was and is offered to all who would overcome. "Tarry ye...until ye be endued with power...."

ABOUT THE AUTHOR

Born in Portland, Oregon, in 1884, Daniel A. Poling represents the fifth generation in an unbroken line of preachers in the Evangelical Church. Soon after graduation from Dallas College in Oregon, in 1904, Dr. Poling was given his first church—in Canton, Ohio. Later, he served briefly as a student pastor in Columbus, Ohio. He then became general and field secretary of the Ohio Christian Endeavor Union, and was successively citizenship superintendent, president's associate, associate president, and president of the International Society of Christian Endeavor, and president of the World's Christian Endeavor Union.

After serving overseas during World War I, Dr. Poling was called as associate preacher of the Marble Collegiate Church in New York City. He became co-minister and then minister of this church, resigning in 1930. In 1936 he became minister of the Baptist Temple in Philadelphia, resigning his pastorate after twelve years.

For more than thirty years Dr. Poling has been editor of *Christian Herald*. During World War II he visited most of the active theaters of war as correspondent, chaplain, or carrying letters of instruction from the President of the United States. The recipient of honorary degrees from a dozen colleges and universities, he has also received many awards, among them the Silver Buffalo of the Boy Scouts of America, the Cross of the Huguenot Society, a War Department citation in 1946 "for outstanding and conspicuous service as an accredited war correspondent" and, in 1947, the United States Medal of Merit "for extraordinary fidelity and exceptionally meritorious conduct." Dr. Poling was the first clergyman to receive this highest civilian award that the nation bestows.

Today a resident of New York City, Daniel Poling actively continues his career as clergyman, editor, author, and radio speaker.